GUIDEPOSTS FOR THE SPIRIT:

Stories of Changed Lives

Guideposts

FOR THE
Spirit

STORIES OF
CHANGED LIVES

EDITED BY PEGGY SCHAEFER

Ideals Publications • Nashville, Tennessee

ISBN 0-8249-4616-2

Published by Ideals Publications
A division of Guideposts
535 Metroplex Drive, Suite 250
Nashville, Tennessee 37211
www.idealsbooks.com

Printed and bound in the U.S.A. by RR Donnelley

Library of Congress Cataloging-in-Publication Data
Guideposts for the spirit : stories of changed lives / edited by
Peggy Schaefer.
     p. cm.
Includes index.
    ISBN 0-8249-4616-2 (alk. paper)
    1. Spiritual life. 2. Celebrities—United States. 3. Life change
events—Religious aspects. I. Schaefer, Peggy.
    BL624 .G85 2003
    291.4'32—dc21

                         2002153656

Publisher, Patricia A. Pingry   Series Designer, Eve DeGrie
Managing Editor, Peggy Schaefer   Book Designer, Marisa Calvin
Copy Editor, Melinda Rathjen

Cover art: front cover painting Arts Uniq; back cover and flap paintings
   © Howard Behrens
Interior art: paintings pages 2, 6, 72, 106, 152, 180, 230 © Howard Behrens;
paintings pages 36, 204 Arts Uniq

10 9 8 7 6 5 4 3 2 1

ACKNOWLEDGMENTS
OSGOOD, CHARLES. "Be Yourself" from *Guideposts*, April 2000. Used by permission
of the author.
   All other stories copyright © by Guideposts, Carmel, NY 10512.

CONTENTS

The Gift of Love

MY OWN APOCALYPSE

MARTIN SHEEN
AS TOLD TO CHARLES-EDWARD ANDERSON

*Martin Sheen's acting career in theater, film, and television spans more than
thirty years and includes his award-winning performance in* The West Wing.

In the summer of 1976, I flew to the Philippines to begin work on a film that, to my way of thinking, was a great step upward in my career. I had a leading role in *Apocalypse Now*. At last—a really important movie for this boy from Dayton, Ohio. From now on it was going to be big parts and a taste of real fame. How was I to know it would nearly be the end of me?

From its inception, *Apocalypse* had all the earmarks of success: Francis Ford Coppola, with his worldwide recognition and glittering record of box-office hits, was at the helm as director; Marlon Brando was the costar; Robert Duvall had a supporting role; and the film's financial budget was way up in the millions of dollars.

I had been assigned the role of Captain Ben Willard, an Army intelligence officer and hit man, who, although on the brink of emotional and psychological collapse, had been ordered by his superiors to travel through war-torn Vietnam into Cambodia, where he was to assassinate an American Green Beret colonel. That colonel, played by Marlon Brando, had, from all appearances, gone mad and was operating his own private renegade and bloodthirsty armies in the wilds of the Cambodian jungles.

Just before the filming of *Apocalypse* began, Janet, my wife of fifteen years, and our four children joined me in the Philippines, where movie set designers had transformed the lush, green tropical vegetation outside Manila into amazingly close replicas of the actual photographs I had seen of Vietnam and Cambodia. For as long as I can remember, I have always taken my wife and family along to live with me during extended periods of time on location. I had never wanted my acting role to get in the way of my being a good husband and father. This time was to be no different.

From the first time I read the script of *Apocalypse*, I was fascinated by the character of Captain Willard. I generally try to create a character I'm portraying in my own image—I would "become" Willard. I had no idea how dangerous this would be, for Willard was emotionally burnt out, insensitive to those around him, uncaring, hard-drinking, overly ambitious, self-centered, and single-purposed. Were these menacing attributes of this on-camera character, coupled with the intensity of my own pursuit of success, beginning to boil over into my off-camera life? Or was I really more like Willard than I wanted to admit?

Janet tried to talk about the growing wrinkles in our relationship and tell me what I was doing to others around me, but I vehemently denied that *anything* was changing—least of all me. Then Janet tried to reason with me that she and the kids didn't mind making *some* sacrifices for my success, but now this role was causing me to lock them out. I was making them more and more miserable. Even Francis Coppola was beginning to find me difficult to deal with, but I couldn't seem to help myself.

Although I was raised in a devout Catholic home, the thought of praying about my family problems never entered my mind. And I wasn't about to go near a church—I had given that up in my mid-twenties.

To understand where all this was taking me, let me explain where and how it all began. First, Martin Sheen is only my acting name. Born and christened Ramon

Estevez, I was the seventh of thirteen children of Francisco Estevez and Mary Ann Phelan Estevez. My father, a Spaniard, met my mother, an immigrant from Ireland, while the two attended citizenship training classes in Dayton, Ohio.

I was eleven years old when my mother died. My father, a factory worker for the National Cash Register Company, never remarried and single-handedly raised us (ten boys and one girl; two boys died in infancy) in a lower-middle-class neighborhood in Dayton. I attended Holy Trinity grade school, run by the Sisters of Notre Dame, and Chaminade, a Catholic high school for boys. Early on, I served in the parish church as an acolyte. It was our life in the church that helped keep our family together.

By the time I was six or seven years old, I was spending hours alone acting out the parts of characters I read about in books. Not until movies came into my young life did I know that what I was doing had a name—acting—and I knew then that I was an actor. Right after high school, I headed for New York to fulfill my dream of becoming a professional actor.

That's where "Martin Sheen" was born. The first name came from Robert Dale Martin, a drama coach and friend in New York. The last name came courtesy of the late radio and TV personality Bishop Fulton J. Sheen, whom I admired and, because of my name change, met in 1965. *Martin Sheen*. The name sounded good, solid, Irish. To my eighteen-year-old mind, Ramon Estevez was too ethnic and would cause me to be typecast.

My career in New York grew gradually, first on the stage, then TV and films. I married Janet, an art student at the New School for Social Research, and our family grew gradually too—three sons, Emilio, Ramon, and Carlos (Charlie), and finally our daughter, Renée, all two years apart.

When the Captain Willard role in *Apocalypse Now* came along, it seemed to be the one big, bright opportunity I had been waiting for. But the grueling work of creating *Apocalypse* went on and on, often on hot, steamy days and sultry, humid nights. Nearly six months into the shooting, my Willard-born attitudes, with all the damage they were doing to my family life, had not changed. Our home was now a hotbed of intense stress and pressure.

Our kids began begging to go back to the United States to live with relatives. Finally, Janet gave in and let them go. Then one day in early March 1977, Janet went into Manila for an overnight stay to make sure we would have a decent hotel when I came the next day for a weekend there.

Late in the evening, I got back to the large rustic cabin we had rented for the duration of the filming. It was a comfortable place, perched on a mountainside and overlooking a volcanic lake. However, like all the other houses in the area, it had no telephone, radio, or TV.

On that March night, I was alone and tired. Shooting the scenes of that day had drained me physically and emotionally. I looked forward to sacking out for the night, but when I went to bed I couldn't sleep.

I lay in bed for a while, then got up and paced wildly around the bedroom floor. I felt strangely clumsy and awkward, and at times it was hard to keep my balance. My breathing grew strained. When I went back to bed, sleep defiantly refused to come. I don't recall how many hours I continued in this state, but it must have been about three in the morning when I began to sweat profusely. A nagging pain crept into my right arm, and I leapt out of bed again. Something was terribly wrong, but I had no idea what.

I started to feel faint and slumped to the floor. Then came a devastating explosion of pain in my chest. It left me too weak to stand up. My breathing became rapid and difficult. I had to get outside for help even though I was aware that outside a windstorm was raging.

I slithered slowly over to the closet and, one by one, yanked down pieces of clothing, then twisted and pulled my way into them as best I could. Another blast of pain hit my chest, and I knew what was wrong—a heart attack, the same thing that had claimed the lives of my mother, father, and two of my older brothers. I knew I was dying.

I began to crawl slowly, agonizingly toward the door. The pain in my arm and chest was making me weak. Sweat poured off my body; I rose awkwardly to my feet and began taking baby steps out the front door. Just outside the house, another blast of pain knocked me to the ground.

The wind was still howling. Towering palm trees were bending near the ground and lightning flittered nervously about the sky, giving the whole area the look of an eerie movie set. But this time it was definitely not a movie. Ramon Estevez/Martin Sheen was dying, and the scene was all too real.

When once more I struggled to my feet, I discovered that my depth perception was failing. I reached for trees and clumps of shrubbery, only to find that they were about fifty feet away. Then my eyesight failed altogether. I yelled weakly for the guards the production company had provided, tripped over something and fell again. My hearing was also weak, but I could feel the wind growing stronger. I couldn't move anymore. That's when I called to God for help.

I don't know how long I lay there before one of the security guards making his rounds spotted me and carried me to the guardhouse station. He laid flat boards across the back of a Jeep and gently placed me on them. Then he drove a bumpy mile and a half down the mountainside to a small village, where a young Filipino doctor had a small clinic. I had come to know the doctor earlier since he had often given first aid and other medical treatment to members of the cast and crew. He found my heart rate was very low and my blood pressure was extremely high. He slipped a glycerin tablet under my tongue. Soon another blurred figure bent over me. It was a priest. "Do you want to make your confession?" he asked in broken English. I tried to answer, but couldn't. He waited a long moment, then began to intone the Roman Catholic last rites.

My last memory before losing consciousness was of being placed aboard one of the helicopters—used as a prop in *Apocalypse*—for a daring flight through the storm to a hospital in Manila.

When I awoke, another blurred figure was bending closely over me. This one was smiling. Janet.

"You're going to make it, babe," she said glowingly, "and remember, it's only a movie. It's only a movie." At that very moment, all that ailed me physically, emotionally, and spiritually began to heal.

Even though I did not physically die that night, the Willard character in me did. My face-to-face confrontation with death and my own human vulnerability purged the need to be an empty celluloid image bent on the accumulation of such things as fame or wealth. I had been shocked into recalling something I had known all along, but had forgotten: that love is the true foundation of happiness. Love of family, love of people, love of God.

In the years since that painful night, Janet, our children and I have grown closer and happier than ever. I have long since returned to my church. I have never forgotten that even though I turned my back on God, in my time of greatest need, He came to find me.

JOURNEY TO HEALTH

ANDY GRIFFITH

Andy Griffith's role as Sheriff Andy Taylor on the TV hit The Andy Griffith
Show *is the best known of his many film and televison roles.*

Each of us faces pain, no two ways about it. But I firmly believe that in
every situation, no matter how difficult, God extends grace greater than
the hardship, and strength and peace of mind that can lead us to a place
higher than where we were before. Let me tell you about one of the hardest times in
my own life, and how I found this to be true.

I had been alone for a long time when I met an extraordinary woman named
Cindi Knight. She had come to Manteo, North Carolina, to be in a production of
The Lost Colony, a summer play in which I had gotten my start several decades
before. Our relationship began as a friendship, but as the months passed, I couldn't
help but notice her strong faith and gentle strength. Did I mention she was also
quite beautiful? Somehow, she fell in love with me. Five years after we met as friends,
we became husband and wife.

When she married me in April 1983, I was not at the pinnacle of my career.
Ageism is rampant in Hollywood, and although I was only in my fifties, work was
getting harder and harder to find.

Cindi had suffered from frequent and major sore throats all of her life. So, shortly
after our marriage, we returned to Los Angeles and went to see a throat specialist, Dr.
Robert Feder. He determined her sore throats were coming from her tonsils and scheduled an operation. Early the next morning we drove over to Cedars-Sinai Medical

Center, and Dr. Feder took out her tonsils. While she was recuperating, I got a bad case of the flu. Not exactly a honeymoon of the rich and famous.

My illness was strange. As I got better, the symptoms of influenza were replaced by pain—terrible, searing pain that ricocheted through my entire body. Cindi and I joked about our invalid status and settled in that Saturday to watch the Kentucky Derby on television.

After the race, when I stood up and took a few steps, I plunged headlong into a nightmare. I was overcome by an all-encompassing pain, and I couldn't feel my feet. I had no control over them and fell to the floor in agony.

We couldn't reach any of our doctors that weekend. Yet I was so desperate for relief from the pain that I took some of the codeine prescribed for Cindi for her throat. It barely made a difference.

On Monday my doctor met us at a local hospital. There, a roomful of doctors attempted to find out what was wrong. For four days they hadn't a clue. Finally they did a spinal tap. When the results came in, the mystery was solved. I had Guillain-Barré syndrome, a rare form of nerve inflammation. The nerves become inflamed and begin to send erroneous and scrambled messages to the brain. In some people it causes little pain but extensive paralysis; in cases such as mine, it causes little paralysis but intense pain.

There are no drugs or surgery to treat Guillain-Barré—so the doctor sent me home. "There is nothing we can do," he said. "You've got to ride it out. I'll prescribe some pain medication, but use as little as possible. Come back in a week."

The following week he said the same thing. And the week after that.

By my next visit I was desperate. If anything, the agony was intensifying. Cindi tried not to let me see her fear, but my physical condition was deteriorating noticeably.

Up to that point, we had seen every doctor and specialist I had ever known.

Nothing was helping, and the pain had become so consuming that there was nothing else in my life.

Then an old friend, Leonard Rosengarten, a psychiatrist, asked if he could come to visit. I didn't want a friend to see how bad off I was, so I took my most potent pain medication just before he arrived.

A handsome, white-haired fellow, Dr. Rosengarten had nearly died from cancer of the esophagus, so he knew a thing or two about pain. He pulled up a chair and sat . . . and sat. He waited until the pain medication wore off and I could no longer hide my agony. Then he went to Cindi.

"I know Andy," he said. "He's a stoic if ever there was one. So if he says he's in this much pain, I know he is. Would you mind if I got involved?"

The next morning, true to his word, Dr. Rosengarten got me into Northridge Hospital Medical Center in Northridge, California. I was admitted onto an entire floor of people fighting their way back from auto accidents, strokes, Guillian-Barré. Here, the specialty was therapy and pain management.

I'll never forget that day. The doctor assigned to my case brought along a medication specialist. The first thing the doctor said was, "We know you're in impossible pain. We're here to help you through it." At those words, Cindi said she saw my body relax. Just to have the severity of my condition acknowledged was the first step on my journey to wellness. The druggist was there to start me on as much medication as I needed, but then I would be weaned off it as I learned to handle the pain in other ways.

The doctors at Northridge Hospital knew that treating pain meant treating the whole person, not just the body. Every day we had classes in biofeedback, which taught us how to use our minds to help control pain. For example, imagining the pain coursing down through your body and out through your toes actually releases endorphins that physically fight pain. But even though my pain was gradually diminishing, my foot still felt lifeless. It was slow-going as I shuffled around.

State of mind is crucial, we were taught. Consequently, we patients were all pulling for one another. I'll never forget looking into the day room one Saturday and seeing a group of stroke patients in a semicircle, with a therapist behind each of them. The patients were passing a ball from one to another. Each time one successfully maneuvered the ball to the person seated next to him, all the therapists cheered wholeheartedly. There wasn't a bored or blasé staff member among them. It was one of the sweetest and most wonderful scenes I had ever witnessed.

One day, the therapist working on me saw one of my toes move. The whole hospital heard about it. Patient after patient, doctor and nurse—they all stopped by my door to say, "We heard the great news! Congratulations!" I was on the mend.

So instead of lying at home, isolated, with nothing to do but dwell on the pain, I was suddenly busy. I was part of a team, pulling not only for myself but for the others on my floor as well. By the time I left the hospital a month later, I was taking eighty-five percent less medication than when I arrived. The pain wasn't as severe, and I was equipped to handle it.

Although I was no longer in the acute phase of my illness, we weren't out of the woods yet. It took me nearly a year to recuperate to the point where I could participate in everyday activities. And it was a rough year. My former manager told Cindi and me that we were virtually broke. We thought life would be easier back in my home state of North Carolina, so we put our Los Angeles house up for sale. But the real estate market was bad, and not one good offer was forthcoming.

As I fought my way back from Guillain-Barré, I never stopped thanking God for the help he had provided me through Dr. Rosengarten, and especially through Cindi. She had married me for better or worse, and all she had gotten was the worse.

At the end of that year, I sat in our unsold house with no bank account to speak of and no work in sight. Not only was I old by Hollywood standards, but I had also been out of the game for a year. That alone is hard to overcome. I was getting physically stronger, but I was depressed. We couldn't sell the house—I didn't know what to do.

Then Cindi came up with an off-the-wall idea. "Maybe it's a *good* thing we couldn't sell the house," she said. "Maybe it was God showing us grace. If we moved to North Carolina now you might indeed never work again. What we need to do is stay here and stoke the fire."

That day, and every day for quite a while, Cindi and I went over to the William Morris Agency at lunchtime and sat in the lobby. My agent and every agent in the building saw us. Everybody talked to us. They invited us to their offices; some invited us to lunch.

The upshot of it was I got roles in four TV movies that year, including *Return to Mayberry* with Don Knotts and Ron Howard, and the pilot for *Matlock*—a show that ended up running for nine years!

During this period, Cindi decided to give up pursuing her own acting career and work with me on mine. I don't know how I would have made it without her.

That was more than a decade ago. Now, though *Matlock* is over, I have a new feature film, and I've recorded an album of my favorite gospel songs. Ageism hasn't left Hollywood, but I hope I'll continue to work.

Guillain-Barré has left me with permanent pain in both feet, but like an unwelcome guest, it isn't so bad when I stop paying attention to it.

Challenges and pain will continue all my life, I know, but with Cindi at my side to remind me to accept God's grace, I'll go forward and continue to work with love and happiness.

DEAR DAD

CAROL LAWRENCE

Carol Lawrence is a Tony-nominated performer whose
Broadway roles include Maria in West Side Story.

*I*t was the last straw. I had just returned home from doing a television special out of town. Mother and Dad, who'd come to California to take care of my two boys while I was away, met me at the door.

As soon as I stepped into the house, mother wrapped her arms around me. "Oh, Carol, we saw the special. You were wonderful!"

As she went on, I watched over her shoulder for Dad, who was standing with the boys. *He* was the one I so wanted to please. He had always been a cool and distant man, but I thought this time, just maybe *this* time, he would give me the support I needed. But no. He simply said, "Nice show, Carol," then turned back to the boys.

I bit my tongue while we put away the luggage. Then I stormed into the kitchen, where Mother was doing what she loved most, cooking for the family. The kitchen was filled with the aroma of sautéed calamari. A lobster sauce simmered on one burner and fresh pasta boiled on another.

"It's still a vendetta, isn't it?" I snapped. "He's still bitter because I didn't become a lawyer!"

Mother looked up from stirring her caramel tapioca pudding and sighed. "No, no, Carol, he's forgotten that long ago. You know your father; he is a quiet man. He finds it hard to show his feelings."

"Then I won't show mine either!" I retorted, slapping the counter. That, I determined, would be it. I had tried too long and hard to get close to the man. It was like trying to get a hug from a lamppost.

It had been that way while I was growing up too. Ours was an old-fashioned Italian family in Melrose Park, a suburb west of Chicago. My father, Michael Laraia, was a strict man who could devastate me with a look, a word of disapproval or, worse, of disappointment. Yet my younger brother and I knew he worked very hard to provide for us. He was village clerk and controller for Melrose Park by day and an insurance man at night. His ambition had been to be a lawyer, but he had been brought up by a tyrannical father. Though Dad had won a full scholarship to college, where he intended to take prelaw, his father refused to let him take it. So it was only natural that Dad had definite plans for Joey and me: we would both become lawyers.

Yet as soon as I could walk, I loved to dance. Mother gave me patent-leather tap shoes and lessons at a local dance studio. From then on, I constantly tapped all those shuffles, flaps, and ball changes, wearing out the kitchen linoleum. Then I danced in the garage, leaving the automatic garage door half open for fresh air. At the sound of footsteps on the sidewalk, I'd flick the switch, the door would rise like a theater curtain, and I'd sing and dance at full power. Passersby would stare open-mouthed at the funny little kid with top hat and cane pouring her heart out. By age thirteen I began performing during summer vacations in local social clubs and later danced in the ballet corps of Chicago's Lyric Opera.

My father tolerated it. "That is all right for now, Carolina Maria," he said one Saturday morning as I accompanied him to a local gas station, where he did the owner's accounting. "But I will be so proud when I can point you out in a courtroom and say, 'That is my *figlia.*'"

I smiled and looked out the window. These Saturday mornings with Dad were so precious that I did not want to break the spell.

When I graduated from Proviso High School with a scholarship to Northwestern University, he was ecstatic. He expected me to take prelaw. Instead, I was named freshman of the year in drama.

The following summer, on a family vacation to New York, I found a spot in a Broadway chorus line. My mother was delighted; my father was crestfallen. He hardly said a word to me. After I found a room, they immediately left for home.

In 1957 I got my big break, singing the lead role of Maria in *West Side Story* on Broadway. From then on, life was a whirl of musicals, television specials, and dramas.

In the meantime, my brother, Joey, became a successful lawyer. I married Robert Goulet. Two sons came along. And even though it seemed my father had finally accepted my career, conversations with him were stiff and formal.

Even during the heartbreak years, when my marriage crumbled and I struggled alone to raise my boys, working harder than ever to make ends meet, Father and I remained coolly polite. It was Mother who heard my anguished cries. Yet even she could not fill that empty space within me. More and more I felt that God had stopped loving me because I had not done everything right. I desperately sought some kind of forgiveness, some kind of relief from the guilt that burdened me.

Though I had drifted away from God through the years, I was suddenly drawn to a local church. There I found a warmth and spontaneity I had never known before. Instead of warning me about God's displeasure, the pastor talked about his unconditional love and reminded us that Jesus told us to love thy neighbor as thyself. And I began to understand I couldn't love anybody in a healthy way until I learned to love and accept myself. I joined a women's prayer group, where I could unload my guilt in confidence without fear of being judged.

Knowing finally that God had forgiven me, with all my faults, I began to look outward. I experienced the unexpected joy of devoting time and effort to understanding others. One morning I was inspired to do something I had never considered before.

As I waited at a gas station, the pungent odor of gasoline triggered memories, and once again I was sitting at my father's side in that Melrose Park gas station long ago. A warmth filled me, and I thought of all those unfortunate people I knew who, estranged from a friend or relative, awaited the other person's gesture of reconciliation. So often it came too late. And I remembered a pastor telling me that when Jesus asked us to forgive others seven times seventy, He meant we should swallow our pride and take the first step. I knew what I must do.

That night I wrote Dad a long letter. Into it I poured all the love of a skinny little girl. I told him how I had idolized him and followed him around like a puppy because he epitomized patience, wisdom, understanding, and uncompromising truth.

"Dad, you always had the answer I needed," I wrote, "or knew how to mend whatever I had broken." I told how I marveled at his struggle from the poverty of immigrant status to the success of a highly respected official and businessman.

"Dad, I'm proud to be your daughter," I wrote, "and everybody else, including Mom and Joey, knows how much I really love you. I just wanted you to know it too." I mailed it that night with a profound sense of relief at having done something I should have done long ago.

Later I booked a concert just outside of Chicago for one special reason: Mother had phoned that Dad's health had become critical. He had been living with cancer for some years, but now it was devastating him. The concert would be the second part of my letter. I prayed he'd be well enough to attend.

When I called home to let my parents know when I would arrive, I asked Mother if I could talk to Dad. He got on the phone.

"Dad, did you get my note?"

"Yes," he said, "thank you for a lovely letter."

A lovely letter? Couldn't he at least . . . ? But no, I couldn't let such a thought deter me from reaching for reconciliation. I had no right to expect an emotional outpouring.

While waiting in the auditorium the night of the concert, I was terribly nervous. I had front-row seats set up with special cushions for Dad. Would he be there? I felt like I was six years old and performing for the very first time. Then I saw him coming, with Mom and Joey. His frail frame was bent slightly forward, his thin white hair shining in the auditorium lights. They sat down in front of me.

The comedy numbers were easy, but when I sang ballads, I had to watch the catch in my throat. The most difficult was the close. I was to blow a final kiss to the audience.

"This has been a special time I'll always cherish and keep deep within my heart," I told the people, "and so until next we meet, please remember that"—the orchestra began to play—"you will be my music."

My father looked into my eyes and nodded his head approvingly.

"You will be my song."

He nodded again.

"You will be my music, to fill my heart with love my whole life long."

And then I saw Dad lift his glasses to brush away a tear, and I had to look away for a second. Then Joey helped my father to his feet, and Dad stood clapping and smiling, tears streaming down his face. As I watched him, I was thankful I had taken that first step toward reconciliation. I threw him a kiss and felt my heart swell.

Finally, after Dad died, I learned how complete that reconciliation was. My sister-in-law told me, "You'll never know how much your letter meant to your father. He was so proud of it and would read it to us over and over again. In truth, he had it memorized." Then she added, "We found your letter in your father's pajama shirt pocket where he always kept it, right over his heart."

I bowed my head. Just where I had always wanted to be.

AN UNSCHEDULED STOP

KARL MALDEN

Karl Malden won an Oscar in 1952 for his
supporting role in A Streetcar Named Desire.

cting was the furthest thing from my mind when I got a back-stage carpentry job at the Goodman Theatre School in Chicago. But one day one of the actors the director needed wasn't around, and I was hastened into a play. Suddenly everything in my life changed. All I wanted was to be an actor—a good one. I'm still working at it.

At the Goodman I met Mona Graham, a pretty girl from Emporia, Kansas. When we were married in 1938, Mona gave up her own dream of becoming a star. "One actor in any family is enough," she said. Before we set out to try to make it on the New York stage, I laid down an ultimatum: "Make it big in five years, or we go back to my hometown of Gary, Indiana."

I had some luck on the New York stage and began pushing hard. Too hard.

Suddenly I became sick with a mysterious ailment and everything came to a sharp halt. For the next six months, I languished in a hospital in Denver, Colorado, all knotted up inside. Maybe Someone was telling me something, but I wasn't listening. While the doctors were trying to figure out why the health of a husky man like me had nose-dived, I was trying to figure out why my career had plummeted.

One day, feeling especially depressed, I told Mona, "I'm like an express train that's been derailed."

"Maybe we're not derailed at all," she said. "Maybe we've just made an unscheduled stop in a pleasant place we'd have never seen if we'd been barreling through. Let's get off the train and rest."

"Suppose I don't make it big?" I asked, not resting at all.

"And suppose you just get enough acting jobs to keep food on the table," Mona quickly replied. "We'll still be together. You'll still be doing what you enjoy doing. Relax, Karl, sometimes you have to stop to keep going."

Then and there I stopped my wild race with ambition. And as soon as I did, the doctors discovered an abscess on my lung, treated it successfully, and I went on with my career. Whatever part I got in theater, film, or television, big or small, was sufficient, and I enjoyed doing it. I don't think all that was coincidence.

Since then, whenever the urge to rush ahead hits me, I slip into whatever church is nearby, and there, in the stillness, I thank God for freeing me from the frustrations of pushing too hard. It's a stop I'd recommend to anybody who wants to keep going.

I DIDN'T GET AWAY WITH IT

ROY ROGERS

Roy Rogers is best known as a singing cowboy;
he appeared with his horse Trigger in nearly one hundred films.

What's wrong with a guy who isn't scared when he nearly breaks his neck filming western pictures but gets the shakes when he has to make a simple speech? For years I asked myself this question.

I was shy from my boyhood days, when we lived on the Ohio River in a three-room houseboat built by my father. Our family—Mother, Dad, and three sisters—later settled on a farm outside Portsmouth, Ohio. Dad worked in a shoe factory, while my sisters and I helped Mother run the farm.

We kids went to a one-room schoolhouse, which was just an even hundred yards from the Baptist Church. I know because we measured it and discovered it a perfect distance for a footrace.

Our shoes came off after the last snow and weren't worn again until fall. To toughen our feet in the spring, we ran barefoot races from school to church over a course of tough corn stubbles. My feet grew skin an eighth of an inch thick on the bottom.

By the time I was ten, I could call a square dance and play the guitar. But to get up and talk in front of a class, or just a few people, would make me take off across the cornfields.

I earned a dollar a week by ploughing corn on neighborhood farms; later I quit school and went to work in the shoe factory to help the family finances. When the family went to visit my sister in California, I fell in love with the far West.

I drove a gravel truck in Lawndale, California, for a while; during the depression, I took any kind of job. I helped build a state highway from Newhall to Castaic; later I joined the "Okies," and picked peaches in the California fruit orchards described in *The Grapes of Wrath*.

During my spare time I practiced on my guitar, hoping that some day I could make a living as a musician and a singer. Three of us formed a musical trio called the Texas Outlaws, but it was rough going. Often, the three of us lived in one room, where sleeping was done by unique arrangement of daybed, couch, and chair. In our travels we often had to go out and shoot rabbits to live.

Then, as often happens to a guy who wanders into Hollywood, I had a lucky break; I got a spot in a picture and my film career started. When my wife died during the birth of our third child, I was faced with a demanding career and the responsibilities of raising three fine children.

The story I want to tell begins several years later. Dale Evans, a film star in her own right, and I had been making pictures together for many years. With the unanimous approval of my children, we were married on December 31, 1948.

We had barely been married a few days when she started one morning with, "It's a beautiful day to go to church!"

Now, I wasn't a stranger to churches. I just hadn't time to get acquainted with very many because of other things I preferred doing. "Honey, I've gotta go see Joe Miller this morning," I said quickly. "Why don't you go ahead without me?"

This was the first excuse I could think of, but with more advance warning I could have done much better. Dale fixed a firm eye on me, and I knew her nimble mind was working overtime. She let me get away with it the first time, but going to church soon became the most important thing there was to do on Sunday.

One night before going to bed, I noticed a new book on my reading table.

"Where did this come from?" I asked, picking up a copy of the Bible.

"Since you lost your old one, I bought it for you this morning," Dale said brightly. She knew that I knew I never had a copy of the Bible, but what can you do with a woman whose mind is made up!

Grace before meals became a regular thing. Dale introduced a type of grace where everyone said a sentence prayer. Cheryl, Linda, and Roy Jr.—the three children of my first marriage—were quick to take part. I would squirm in my chair a little, hoping they wouldn't notice me. So it went around the table, then Linda would pipe up, "Why don't you say something, Daddy?"

Dale, God bless her, is the smartest and most loving woman in the world. She didn't press me; but she never lets go of an idea she thinks is right.

Later, when I tried to explain my feelings to Dale, she would say, "The Lord gave you many talents, Roy. Some you use well for yourself, but there are some you haven't developed at all for him. If you could learn to let God speak through you, honey, you could make a good speech every time—and not die doing it."

I didn't know what she meant at first. To some people, religion may come in one big emotional experience. I moved to it a step at a time: regular attendance at church, reading a few passages from the Bible, saying grace. A warm quality grew in our family life. It was a spiritual kind of love that makes you want to do something for others.

A group of people in Hollywood began to get together and talk about all these things—Tim Spencer, Red Harper, Colleen Townsend, Jane Russell, Henrietta Meers, Connie Haines, Joyce Compton, Dale, myself, and others. We would meet at different homes, some of us bringing along extra chairs. There was prayer for the problems of others; several would speak of religion out of their own experience.

I never had enough education to understand theology, but when a fellow like Tim Spencer stands up before a group like this and tells frankly how his belief in

Jesus Christ helped him change from a drunk to a hard-working citizen, then Christianity comes alive for me.

One day I discovered that I actually looked forward to saying the blessing at mealtime. It may sound corny, but I could hardly wait for my turn. I began to appreciate the wholesome things that happen in each area of life when you're right with God. Not that I don't have plenty far to go.

As I said before, Dale is a mighty smart woman. She helped bring something new into our family life, but not at the sacrifice of other things we enjoyed, like outdoor sports.

The biggest triumph came when I used Dale's suggestion about speaking in public. The occasion was like many others. The music part I handled without any fear, but when it came time to say a few words, I felt the same old nervous symptoms. Then I closed my eyes for just a moment and said silently, "Lord, I'll just make a mess of things on my own. Help me to relax a little so that what I say to these people will really mean something."

I started to talk and found myself saying things I'd never said before. And they came out as naturally as if I were just standing there and someone else was talking. From that time on, I've never had more than the normal amount of nervousness.

Somehow it doesn't make any difference now whether the group is simple farm folks or sophisticated New Yorkers; the things I try to say are the same. At the rodeo in Madison Square Garden, I took the opportunity at every performance to reply to a letter I received from a boy who asked, "Is it sissy to go to Sunday school?"

Now there was a question I really enjoyed answering.

"It certainly is not," I said. "Going to Sunday school and church is one of the greatest privileges we have. I only wish I had been smart enough to know this earlier in my life."

SHE'S MY WOMAN

RANDY TRAVIS

*After years of success as a country singer, Randy Travis released
his first Christian music album,* Inspirational Journey, *in 2000.*

Country music isn't famous for its stable relationships. At least that's
what most people think. But look at me—I've been married to the same
woman for ten years now, and I've known her for twenty-five. My relationship with Lib has helped me find my way many times. What's best, though, is
that it finally led me to the most important relationship in my life—my relationship with God.

I count myself blessed now; in my younger days I never would have imagined
such a thing was possible. After all, I had grown up hearing stories about country
stars having affairs and getting divorces. I knew songs like "Your Cheatin' Heart"
and "Don't the Girls All Get Prettier at Closing Time." And I had lived the life
myself, playing in bands with Ricky, my older brother. We sang all around our
hometown of Marshville, North Carolina—at VFW halls, Moose lodges, private
parties, wherever we could. When I was just seventeen, settling down and getting
married was the furthest thing from my mind. All I cared about was whatever would
get me through the night.

That was before I walked into Country City USA, a music club in Charlotte,
North Carolina. I was sitting at one of the tables when a blond woman, who was all
of five-feet-nothing, came up and sat down. "I'm Lib Hatcher," she said, "and I own
this place." I liked her from the get-go. And she liked my singing.

But there wasn't much for her to like about me. I was out of control—a messed-up high school dropout who had been drinking and using drugs every single day since the age of fourteen. The police in Marshville knew me for the juvenile delinquent I was. Once, when I was blind drunk, I stole my brother's car and totaled it. The policeman who hauled me in said he had clocked me going 145 miles per hour. I was arrested again, for breaking into a store in Marshville. It was a dumb thing to do, and this time it was serious. Already on probation, I would now have to appear before a judge. I was looking at jail time, and I was scared. The way I was living, I was headed for jail or the local cemetery.

About the only thing I had going for me was that I could sing. But so what? So could lots of guys. To me it was just a way to have some fun and make a little money. That's what brought me to Country City in the first place. It was one of two big clubs in town, and they were holding a talent contest. I'd been thinking of entering, but after meeting Lib, my decision was pretty much made for me. Not only that, but I ended up winning the contest. "How 'bout singing here regularly?" Lib asked. Soon enough I was onstage five nights a week.

One night at the club I was thinking about that upcoming date with the judge. Lib asked what was bothering me; it was just like her to notice. She watched over her employees all the time.

"Well, I have to go to court in a few days," I confessed. I hated having to admit it to her, but Lib was the kind of person you could never slip anything past.

I was surprised when she answered, "I'll go there and stand up with you."

Lib followed through on her promise and showed up at court with me. "Randy," my lawyer said, "I've gotten you out of trouble before, but I don't know about this one. You're looking at five years."

I felt like throwing up. I walked into that courtroom fully expecting to spend my next five birthdays in the penitentiary. Lib was with me, though, and that helped me breathe a little easier. Still, I didn't expect her to do what she did.

As the proceedings came to an end, Lib spoke up. "Your Honor," she told the no-nonsense judge, "this young man is working for me full-time as a singer in my club. He's got a future and I'll vouch for him. I run a respectable establishment." She said her piece in that same sort of straight-shooting way that had made me like her in the first place.

The judge took stock of Lib, then gave me a good long stare before he said, "Son, I'm going to let you go one more time. But if you ever appear before me again, you'd better bring along a toothbrush. 'Cause you're gonna stay a while."

You're one lucky man, I thought. Leaving the courthouse, I realized it wasn't luck. It was Lib. That made me think that maybe she saw more in me than I saw in myself.

I found out how true that was one night at the club after I'd finished my set. Lib came over and said, "Randy, we need to talk." She led me to a quiet spot in a corner and sat me down. "Have you ever considered making singing a career?" she asked.

I had never thought much about my future—to me it was high times all the time—but it was obvious Lib had. And I knew she wasn't the type of person to say things she didn't believe. "Maybe I could try," I allowed. "But I'm not good at business."

"I am," Lib said. "I run this place all right, don't I?" And that's how she became my manager.

The first thing she did was to get me into a recording studio. We made a demo tape of some songs and shopped it around. Not a single major record label was interested. "Sounds nice," they would say, "but it isn't gonna sell." The traditional country I played wasn't what listeners wanted. People in those days were into pop-country, crossover stuff, thanks in part to the movie *Urban Cowboy*. Finally, in

1979, a little label called Paula Records, out of Shreveport, Louisiana, agreed to take a chance and release the single "She's My Woman."

Lib and I loaded a car full of the records and drove up and down the East Coast, going from radio station to radio station to talk deejays into playing my song. Loretta Lynn and her husband did the same thing, I thought during one of those drives. The word "husband" stuck in my head, and I started looking at Lib with a different kind of affection. She must've seen it in my eye, because she'd give me a big old smile whenever she caught me looking at her that way.

Our road trip paid off. Stations started playing my song, and it even got onto the country charts. Then interest in my music seemed to fizzle.

My interest in Lib only grew. She felt the same way about me and would not give up on my career, even though I had some moments when I was ready to. She wasn't the type. I couldn't let down a woman like that, so I vowed to straighten up. I finally quit drinking and drugging and started taking my music a lot more seriously.

Even though Charlotte was a fine place for me to be, Lib knew that we needed to move to Nashville if I was going to make it in the music business. She got a manager for Country City. We moved to Nashville in 1981 with no jobs and very little money. We drove back to North Carolina on weekends to check the club, and I would sing. Finally, she got an offer to manage a club in Nashville in 1982.

Lib put me to work singing, cooking, and washing dishes in the club. Every night, I'd finish up my work in the kitchen, then get onstage. I developed a following around town, and thanks to the success of fellows like Ricky Skaggs and George Strait, my type of "roots" country was becoming popular again. In 1985, I got signed to Warner Bros. Records, where I recorded *Storms of Life*. The first single from the album, "1982," became a hit. The album was a staggering success, the first country debut to sell a million copies within a year of issue. I won the Academy of

Country Music's "Top New Male Vocalist" award. My career was thrown into high gear, and I had a string of hits. I released four albums by 1990, and each one went platinum.

The following year, Lib and I were married. I had asked her to marry me because there was nothing that I wanted more than to be with her. Except maybe to be more like her. She saw the good things in people, and I was beginning to figure out why.

Lib went to church regularly with some old friends in Nashville, and I started tagging along. I always thought that if I got too much religion, I would lose the old Randy Travis. Then one day, I asked myself, "Has Lib ever steered you wrong?" So, like Lib, I started reading the Bible and praying and trusting in God. And you know what? I found it made me more like myself, my good self. The self Lib had seen buried inside a scruffy, messed-up kid who'd wandered into her club all those years ago, one mistake away from prison.

I'm not saying I'm perfect. I'm far from it, as I see every day. But now I know that as much as I need Lib, I need God more. My growing relationship with him is what led me to record *Inspirational Journey*, my first gospel album.

Not too long ago, I asked Lib, "Is this what you had in mind when we first met?"

"Nope," she said, taking my hand. "But Someone else must have had it in mind."

Someone who helped me see in myself what he has known all along.

Words of Encouragement

WITH A LITTLE HELP FROM MAMA

REBA MCENTIRE

*In addition to her singing career, Reba McEntire
has also established herself as a talented actress.*

It was a beautiful spring morning when Mama and I set out from our ranch in Oklahoma for Nashville, Tennessee, where I was going to audition for a recording contract. I was twenty years old, well prepared vocally, and ready to take a chance on the dream of a lifetime.

As the hillsides rolled by, resplendent with dogwood and redbud blossoms, I felt a creeping uneasiness. The closer we got to the country music capital, the more I tried to prolong the trip, making Mama detour for some sightseeing, then for a snack, then for anything I could think of. Finally I yelled, "Stop!" and Mama pulled the big blue Ford into a Dairy Queen on the side of the highway and we went inside.

As I toyed with my mountain of ice cream, I didn't have to explain that I was scared. Mama knew me too well. "Reba Nell," she said, adding the *Nell* for gentle emphasis, "we can turn around right now and go on back home if that's what you want, and I'll understand. The music business is not for everyone."

I looked at Mama across the melting swirl of my sundae. She wasn't pushing me. But when she was my age, Mama would have given just about anything to have had the opportunity I had now. I wondered if that was what was confusing me.

We'd always had a special bond. Maybe it was because of my singing. Music had always been a part of Mama's life. But right out of high school she had to take a teaching job, working in a two-room schoolhouse. Then she married, worked as an assistant to the school superintendent, and did all the bookkeeping on our ranch while raising four kids.

Mama and I were middle kids, both the third of four children. Being a middle kid, I was always looking for attention. I was a tomboy, doing everything my older brother, Pake, did. "Anything you can do I can do better!" was our sibling motto, whether it was throwing rocks and doing chin-ups, or riding horses and roping. I was out to be the best, to get the attention. Then I learned to sing.

I remember that in the second grade, my music teacher, pretty Mrs. Kanton, helped me learn "My Favorite Things" from *The Sound of Music*. When I went home and sang it for Mama, her eyes met mine and just sort of glowed. It tickled me to think I could make Mama react like that, and to hear adults say that I was gifted.

That's what my grandmother—Mama's mother, who I was named after—used to say when I was growing up. But she called it a special gift, a gift from God. I was almost as close to her as I was to Mama. Grandma used to take me fishing at a pond on her place. We never did catch much, but we liked to throw in our lines and sit on the pond dam while Grandma told stories, mostly from the Bible. She told me about David, Moses, and Daniel, and the special gifts that God had given them, like courage and leadership and prophecy. In fact, David was a songwriter.

I probably learned as much of the Bible going fishing with Grandma as I did in Sunday school. She taught me gospel songs and hymns so I could sing to her. "Reba," she'd say, "God gives all of us our own special gifts, and He's given you yours for a reason. Now you have to learn to use it."

The cherry was sliding down the whipped cream peak on my sundae. I looked outside at the glowing Dairy Queen cone rotating slowly, almost as if it were sitting on a record turntable. Mama was nursing a cup of coffee and watching the traffic flash by. She was not about to rush me.

We'd spent many an hour on the road together. Grandpap and Daddy were champion steer ropers. During summers we'd all go with Daddy on the rodeo circuit. We had a two-horse trailer that was so heavy that all four of us kids had to stand on the back of it so Daddy could pull the nose up and hitch it to the Ford. Then we'd pile into the back seat and take off for rodeos in Wyoming and Colorado. We'd play road games, like counting mile markers or Volkswagens. We'd see who could spot the most out-of-state license plates.

Then someone would strike up a song and everybody would join in. Mama coached. She kept us on pitch and taught us how to harmonize. If the lyrics got lost in the jumble, she announced, "Okay, stop. Reba Nell, *enunciate*. Now go ahead." One word would do it. That was the schoolteacher coming out in her.

When we got older, Pake, my younger sister Susie, and I formed a country and western band at Kiowa High School. We called ourselves the Singing McEntires. We practiced in the living room while Mama was in the kitchen frying potatoes. I remember one day we were singing harmonies and things got a little messed up. I was on Susie's part or Susie was on Pake's—we couldn't tell—but Pake got really aggravated and started bossing us around. Soon enough, Mama marched in, spatula in hand. "All right," she said, "sing it."

We sang it.

"Susie, you're on Reba's part," she said, pointing with her spatula. "Now, just sing the song." We sang it.

"That sounds better. Sing it again." We sang it again.

"That's perfect. Now do it once more." Then she walked back into the kitchen. That was Mama.

Across the Formica tabletop I caught Mama glancing at her watch. I couldn't stall much longer. My ice cream had turned to soup.

After my voice had matured into a real singer's instrument, I started performing at rodeos. I loved singing to the big crowds. I'd listen to my favorite country music stars, like Loretta Lynn and Dolly Parton, and go out there and try to sound just like them and get all that attention. Then one day Mama took me aside for a quiet talk that would turn out to be one of the most important conversations we ever had.

"Reba Nell," she said, "you have a beautiful voice all your own. If people want to hear Dolly or Loretta sing, they'll buy their albums. But now you've got to find your own style. Sing what you feel, sing from your own heart, and you'll discover the voice God intended for you. That's what people will really come to hear."

She was right. After our talk, people in the music business started taking a good look at me, and that's why we were now sitting here in this Dairy Queen outside Nashville.

I looked up at Mama. She was fishing in her purse for the keys to the Ford. "Reba," she said, pulling them out, "I'm serious about turning back. If you get that record deal, I'll be very proud of you. But if you don't, I'll be just as proud." Then she reached over and gave me a tight hug, and suddenly I remembered the glow in her eyes when I sang "My Favorite Things."

I knew what that glow had meant. All Mama wanted—all any mother wants for her child—was for me to be myself. And she'd seen what I could be. She didn't have to say that if I signed a record deal she'd be living out her dreams a little bit through me. I understood that now and I was proud. Suddenly I wanted to get to Nashville as quickly as we could.

And I've been making records ever since, using those gifts that Grandma talked about and Mama helped me find: The gifts God provides to make each of us unique.

ALL OF US NEED TO BELONG

BILLY MILLS

*Billy Mills, an Oglala Sioux Indian, won the gold medal
for the 10,000-meter race in the 1964 Summer Olympics in Tokyo.*

In the spring of 1974, I went back to Pine Ridge looking for answers. I stood on the dusty road that runs through the prairie town into the rolling Black Hills of South Dakota and squinted in the morning sun at the tiny ramshackle house where I'd spent the first twelve years of my life. I had fought hard to leave the poverty of our reservation, and I had. Like other members of minority groups who make it outside their home turf, I was truly grateful for what I now had: a loving wife, three precious daughters, and a comfortable home. Yet, I still felt a restlessness at the core of my being. This feeling had driven me here, back to my heritage, to look for something to ease the loneliness I was feeling.

This sleepy South Dakota town on the Pine Ridge Indian Reservation had not changed much in twenty years. The small board houses were still dwarfed by the wealth of nature surrounding them. I'd lived here with my mother, who was three-quarters French and one-quarter Indian; my father, a Lakota (Sioux) man; and my brothers and sisters and relatives. Sometimes we numbered as many as fifteen in our four-room house. I hardly remember my mother, who died when I was small, but I can never forget my father, a stocky muscular man with straight dark hair and a gentle, weathered face.

Dad had a fierce love for all of his children, but I felt there was a special connection between him and me. Now, standing in front of this small house, I pictured the year I was twelve years old. I saw the two of us as we walked home from church in the early morning: him broad-shouldered and proud in a dark tie and a white shirt, and me, a barely awake youngster in T-shirt and jeans. Since his stroke, he'd run a barbershop out of our house, and my favorite time of day was helping him set up for the day's business. I'd sweep the floor while he sharpened his shiny barber's scissors. And we'd talk. There wasn't anything I couldn't tell him.

All of us need to belong, yet even as a child I felt I didn't fit anywhere. "The white people don't want me," I'd complain to Dad. "To them I'm an Indian, and they have signs up in their town: 'No dogs or Indians allowed.' And they won't serve us in their restaurants. And my Lakota classmates, well . . ." I paused, embarrassed, "they say the only thing worse than a Wasicu [white man] is an Ieska [half-blood]. I wish I was one thing or the other. But I'm nothing. I don't fit anywhere."

Dad never tried to placate me. Instead he'd try to find practical solutions for my feeling of not belonging. "Billy," he said to me more than once, "you can learn to be good at sports. It's a way to compete in white society." He must have seen the look on my face. We both knew I wasn't a natural athlete.

Or he would say, "It will be a struggle, son, to find a place in the white world— or to earn the respect of your father's people—but it is possible to walk in two worlds with one spirit. This, however, you must always remember: You are my son, and you belong. You belong to me."

I believed that I belonged to him and took strength from that knowledge. But that frail cord of acceptance snapped one morning several weeks later while Dad was cutting hair. He suffered another stroke and was taken to the hospital. That night when my sister told me he was dead, I ran out the creaking back door, over the hills, as far as my legs could carry me. I don't remember anything about the next two days.

But two things had changed: I now felt completely alone. And I'd started running.

I continued running at Haskell, one of the Indian boarding schools where my brothers and sisters and I were sent since there was no one at home to care for us. I would run five or ten miles on weekends, because it allowed me to get away from everybody else. And I just cried. I'd be crying while I was running. A half-blood and an orphan—you couldn't feel much lonelier than that.

Before long, running, my means of escape, became my means of acceptance. I won a track scholarship to a predominantly white university. After graduation I earned a commission in the Marine Corps. Eventually, on October 14, 1964, the world was astounded at the Tokyo Olympics when I won the gold medal for the 10,000-meter race.

Dad had been right that day thirteen years earlier. Through sports I'd won acceptance and respect. The Lakota people gave me Warrior status and an Indian name. Makocé Terila (Respects-the-Earth). These were honors usually reserved for full-bloods. I'd married Pat, the woman I loved, who was white, and we settled in a beautiful community outside Sacramento, California. I had a good job selling insurance. I wanted to make sure that others wouldn't be left destitute because of a death, the way my own family had been. Things were going well. I should have been content.

So why was I standing here in front of this now-dilapidated house in Pine Ridge? I had thought that this long-sought acceptance would finally give me a sense of belonging. Instead there was a vacuum in the center of me. Was it that, even though two cultures accepted me, I knew I wasn't truly one or the other? *I* knew I didn't belong. Somehow I had hoped that by coming back to my roots, back to where I was born, I could find some answer to my restlessness. So Respects-the-Earth had come back.

As had happened before, when I first arrived at the reservation, I felt a fleeting sense of peace. At first I saw what I wanted to see: the ancestral land of a proud, strong people. So much of what I'd learned here was right: respect for the earth, for one's elders, for wisdom, for the culture of hundreds of generations now gone. But when my eyes adjusted, I saw the struggle of Pine Ridge: once, we had been a people at home here. We had a spiritual grounding in this country and knew that the Black Hills were "the heart of everything there is." But promises had shattered, treaties had been broken. The Black Hills had been illegally taken away. Now the reservation meant inadequate housing, improper medical care, splintered families. The spirit of our people was imprisoned. There was poverty and despair.

Like other Lakota facing this struggle, I knew this place itself was not the answer to my heart's cry to belong.

I had come to the end of my resources. I needed someone wiser than myself. "Oh, Dad," I said, "you had such wisdom. Why aren't you here to tell me the secret of your serenity? How did you find peace in the face of need and ill health?"

Of course, Dad wasn't here. But another very wise man was—Fools Crow, an elder and spiritual leader of our tribe. I felt a new hope mixed with trepidation at the idea of an audience with him, but I knew I had to go.

While the honored citizens of many cultures have mansions and fancy cars, Fools Crow chose to live simply in a log cabin, miles from anywhere.

There was a tranquility inside the small house. Fools Crow was past seventy and his chestnut skin was weathered, but he still stood tall and his eyes shone with an ageless vitality. He received me and invited me to sit down. "I am troubled," I started. "There are questions to which I cannot find answers."

All of my frustrations came pouring out: my need to know where I truly belonged. How I'd looked everywhere and hoped to find my answer here. How the yearning still hadn't gone away.

"Billy," he started, speaking in Lakota, "I think you are still troubled that you are

Ieska. But that is not the cause of your restlessness. Many of our people, full-bloods, go to the city as you did. Look what happens: many of them drink, fight, become lost—lost souls. So they come back here, and what are they doing? Fighting, drinking. Their souls are lost here as well. The reservation is not the answer. A place does not give peace. So, what is the answer to this yearning?"

He paused and looked squarely at me. "The answer you seek lies with your Creator. Lakota, white, black—the Great Mysterious Creator made us all. There are two roads in life, the black road and the red road—the spiritual road. We are made with a yearning to walk the spirit road with our Creator. When you are on the spirit road, you may journey through any country in peace."

The burning in my chest told me he was right. This was his secret and this had been Dad's secret as well. God, the Great Mysterious Creator, had been Dad's strength, his center. This is why he had taken me to church, why he began each day in worship. Dad had counseled me to "walk in two worlds with one Spirit." Yet, I hadn't taken much time for God, for the "red road."

"Fools Crow," I said, "my father worshiped the Christian God. My daughters are in Catholic school. Am I turning my back on my heritage to worship this way?"

"Billy," he said gently, "there is one God. You honor your people in worshiping him the way you know to be true."

A chilly wind parted the grasses as I left Fools Crow's cabin. But as I stood in the silence of the prairie, looking toward the Black Hills, I heard a familiar answer to my plea for acceptance, this time from a Father even greater than my own: *You are my son, and you belong. You belong to me.*

I started down the dirt road. For the first time, I wasn't running away from, or toward, anything. I was running *with* my God, my Creator. And no matter where my earthly journey takes me, I know Billy Mills is already home.

MR. ELECTRICO

RAY BRADBURY

Among Ray Bradbury's many science fiction titles are
The Martian Chronicles *and* Fahrenheit 451.

The longer I live, the more I see how God often touches our lives through other people. I'll never forget that magical autumn afternoon when he used Mr. Electrico to touch mine. It happened when I was twelve, in my hometown of Waukegan, Illinois, on Lake Michigan's shore.

It was the kind of golden September day when the last of summer touched the land while the autumn wind promised winter. It was also the day when the Dill Brothers Combined Traveling Shows came to town.

To me, the Dill Brothers Shows might as well have come from Katmandu, the other side of the moon, or the outer rings of Saturn. As soon as their gasoline generators coughed awake and the calliope's chords drifted over the seared fields, I dashed headlong toward this faded and patched canvas wonderland.

I ran so hard I tasted iron, and my heart exploded as I arrived at the sideshow where I stared open-mouthed at Mr. Electrico. A towering, hawk-nosed figure with a fiery stare that put out your eyes, he spoke in tones I felt proclaimed God's truth. With a flourish of his black cape, he ensconced himself in a wondrous electric chair, and an assistant threw a switch and proclaimed, "Here go ten million volts of pure fire, ten million volts of electricity into the flesh of Mr. Electrico!"

As the current surged through his body, his white hair billowed into a bright halo, his body seemed to glow, and incandescent fire danced at his fingertips. I watched mesmerized as he picked up a silver sword, leaned down, and touched *me* with it on both shoulders, then the tip of my nose. The electricity surged through me, making *my* hair stand on end. He shouted, *"Live forever!"*

I fell back stunned. His words filled my ears like a divine command. I did not know that the electricity used in such performances was of low amperage and harmless, but I did know that something incredible was happening to me.

The next day, even while attending an uncle's funeral, I could not forget Mr. Electrico. As our car headed home for the family's post-funeral wake, to my parents' consternation I leaped out and raced down the hill to the carnival. I carried with me, as an excuse to see Mr. Electrico, a ball-in-vase trick I had ordered through the mail from Johnson Smith & Co. I *had* to find out just how to "Live forever!" How did it fit with what I'd learned Sundays at my Baptist church? I sensed that we could live on with God after we died, but Mr. Electrico's proclamation indicated something different.

I found him wandering thoughtfully among the tents. He seemed happy to see me and offered to introduce me to his fellow performers. Before we entered, he slapped the side of the faded tent with his cane and cried out, "Clean up your language!"

The sideshow folks "cleaned up their language," and he ushered me in and introduced me to the Skeleton Man, the Fat Woman, the Illustrated Man, and the Bearded Lady. Then we walked out to the sandy shore of Lake Michigan, where we sat on a log. He talked his small philosophies and let me talk my big ones.

It was a long conversation that lasted until the lake horizon melted into dusk. What were my goals? What was the meaning of my life? As we talked, I discovered he had been a Presbyterian minister. As I was to learn, he was still ministering.

He spoke of how important it was for us to be true to what we had been given to do in life. And on that log I began to realize just what he meant by "Live forever!" He wasn't referring to salvation. His emphasis was on the word *live*. He was saying that this life, too, was sacred and must be lived to the fullest. Each day, each hour was precious. Each of us must make the most of every moment to use the gifts God had given us.

As I listened to Mr. Electrico, I realized that a few years before, I had almost discarded the gift God had given me. At age nine the call of distant planets had excited my imagination. I had carefully cut out Buck Rogers comic strips from our local newspaper. But when the kids in school learned about it they made fun of me. I tore them up in embarrassment. A month later I burst into tears and wondered why I was crying. Who had died? *Me!* For I had listened to those fools who couldn't understand my gift or my need for the influence of Buck Rogers in shaping my future. I went back to collecting him. I was made whole again.

Something happened to me as Mr. Electrico and I talked through that warm autumn afternoon. His blazing sword had truly fired my imagination and made me fully realize what my calling in life was.

Though I had done some writing, after my encounter with Mr. Electrico, I began to write faithfully every day. I asked for and got a Simplex toy typewriter from my parents for Christmas. It took hours to compose a single paragraph on the machine, dialing letters on a rubber disc and pressing them one by one against the paper. But I wrote all of my first stories with the wondrous gift.

Since that one bright afternoon with Mr. Electrico, I have never stopped writing. Thus I celebrate the gift God has given me. I believe each of us has such a talent to put to work to find ourselves, and, in the finding, we help others. Some ignore their talents; some let friends talk them out of their gifts as not being "practical." Sadly, too many forgo their inherent genetic ability in the mindless pursuit of money.

I'll never forget the taxi driver I once met in New York; he took great joy in celebrating his gift. He was a joy to ride with because he madly loved his cab. It must have been thirty years old, but he kept it polished so that it blazed. When we reached our destination, he jumped out to lift the hood and proudly displayed its motor. It was all silver-chromed; he had burnished every part by hand. As the engine purred between us like a huge contented cat, I looked up at him to see a delighted, fulfilled man.

He knew how to live. Somewhere, long ago, he had met *his* Mr. Electrico!

Game Plan

Pee Wee Kirkland

Pee Wee Kirkland, a former NBA draft pick by the Chicago Bulls, founded the School of Skillz in order to help young people avoid the mistakes he had made.

ome sounds you never forget. I remember first hearing the *slap-slap-slap* of a basketball on the streets of Harlem when I was eight years old. I loved it right away—like a great song. My father, Joseph, was a fan of baseball, and he wanted me to be a shortstop. But I couldn't tear my eyes away from the kids shooting hoops, and finally I picked up a ball. It was like magic in my hands. At the playground at the Milbank Community Center on 118th Street, I saw guys forever practicing moves I could make in ten minutes. That's when I knew I had a gift.

Back then, in the mid 1960s, Roger "Buster" Bryant, the coach at Milbank, was every kid's inspiration, and I wanted to make him proud. "You've got a bright future, Pee Wee," he told me one day. Then he warned me that some of the older guys would be after me, trying to lead me astray. "If they do, keep it outside this gate," he said, pointing to the playground entrance. Buster believed the basketball court was sacred ground, a place we could come for refuge from the streets and to discover the better parts of ourselves.

My mother, Mary, felt the same way about church, and she made sure to take me and my brothers to services every week. I usually squirmed beside her in the pew, itching to be back outside at Milbank, perfecting my moves. One Sunday she pulled me close. "When you start listening," she whispered, "your whole life will change."

I didn't get what she was trying to tell me, not then. I was too young, and what the older kids had to teach me seemed more interesting at the time. They taught me to play craps for money, and I liked the sound of dice rattling on the sidewalk. Before I knew it, I was hooked.

I was tired of the ghetto life. I wore the same shirt to school every day, saw my parents break their backs to put food on the table, and heard my mother crying because they had no presents for us at Christmas. "God," I used to pray, "if you're as powerful as my mother says, make me a force so I can help my family. I want something bigger and better for them."

For a boy growing up in Harlem in those days, the biggest thing in the world was basketball. We all played at Rucker Park on 155th Street and Frederick Douglass Boulevard. NBA stars came up there to test their skills against the street legends, guys like Joe "The Destroyer" Hammond, "Jumpin" Jackie Jackson, and Frank "Shake and Bake" Streety. By the time I was in my teens, Pee Wee Kirkland had become a name too. I was the only player in high school scoring fifty points in a game. They called me "Stickman," because I had so many moves I made the other guys look like they were stuck to the court.

Pretty soon I came to understand the money game as well as I understood basketball. Before I graduated from high school, I graduated from petty crime to the big time, lending money for drug deals. It was okay, I told myself, because I was only doing it to get my folks out of the ghetto. And I did. I moved them out of Harlem to a nice house on Long Island.

I thought I had made it. Still, I knew my parents—especially my mother—would be deeply disappointed in me if they ever found out how I came by my money. So I tried to go legit. I was running the fast break at Norfolk State University when the NBA offered me a forty-thousand-dollar contract with the Chicago Bulls in 1968. I went to Chicago, only to have the coach promote another rookie. Maybe he went to a school with a bigger name, but I knew I was the better player. To me, that wasn't what basketball was about. I quit and went home to New York.

It didn't take long before people from the old days came to me. "Get us a hundred thousand dollars," they said, "and we'll give you a hundred and fifty at the end of the month." I had given up crime when I went to college, but now I didn't have a job and I needed to make a living. So I got into moneylending—and the fast life—again.

In 1970 my wrongdoings caught up with me. I was arrested on charges of conspiracy to sell drugs. If anybody deserved to go to jail, it was Pee Wee Kirkland. I just wasn't guilty in *that* particular case. The warrant had been issued from Boston, where I had never been in my life; but a witness pointed me out in court, and I was sentenced to fifteen years. Later I said to the district attorney, "You know I wasn't guilty." He agreed, then added, "But it's not like you had a nine-to-five, Pee Wee."

His words stuck with me after I was sent to Lewisburg Federal Penitentiary in Pennsylvania. In prison I didn't have wads of cash, fancy cars, or expensive houses anymore. I had nothing. Nothing but plenty of time to sit in my cell and think.

I took a long, hard look at myself, and I wasn't proud of what I saw. That district attorney was right. Here I was, a grown man, and I had never bothered to make an honest living. Instead I took the easy way out and let down everyone who believed in me. My old coach, Buster, my father, my mother—especially Mom.

Then I heard her voice, gentle yet firm, as she said to me in church so long ago, "When you start listening, your whole life will change." Suddenly it was crystal clear what she had been trying to tell me. It wasn't just that she expected better from me. *God* expected better from me. To truly live, I had to listen to him, to do what he wanted me to do. I had to let him show me the plan he had for my life.

The best way to gain that wisdom, I figured, was to go back to the beginning, to where I had felt the clearest sense of purpose: the basketball court. I began doing in prison what Buster had done for me on the playground—trying to teach the younger guys not just the game, but also teamwork and self-respect. And I started reading the Bible, as I had seen my mother do for all those years. Hearing the slap of the ball as I dribbled downcourt during a prison-yard game and really listening to the Word of God for the first time, I felt like I was headed in the right direction again.

Shortly after I was released from prison in 1988 (after serving a second sentence, for tax evasion), I met and married a wonderful woman, KleoPatra. We made our home in Brooklyn, New York, her old neighborhood; and both of us kept praying for God's design to continue unfolding.

One day I saw a kid shooting baskets with his father at a playground near our house. "Are you teaching him the game?" I asked.

"I'm trying," his dad admitted, "but I don't really know it myself."

I showed the kid, Sweetwater, the basics. That boy loved basketball. Even when it was freezing he was outside working on his jumper, and I would put on my gloves and join him.

By 1990 my work with Sweetwater had grown into a program called the School of Skillz, with the support of Nike and Manhattan's Central Baptist Church, whose pastor, Reverend Faulkner, let us use the church gym. I wanted to teach kids from Harlem the skills they needed to do well—on and off the court. If I could help even one of them avoid making the mistakes I had made, then I could feel like I had finally done something to make my mother and Buster proud.

In 1996 I started working with another group of kids. Reverend Faulkner introduced me to Stephen Spahn, chancellor of the Dwight School in Manhattan, who offered me a job as basketball coach. The guys on the Dwight team came from backgrounds different from the kids I worked with in the School of Skillz, but my goals for them were the same: be good people first, then good ballplayers.

In 1997 our team won the private school state championship. I was happy for the kids and the school, and, yes, I was excited about winning. Still, as the final buzzer went off, I caught my wife's eye across the court. Then I thought about my mother cheering us on at home, and I knew that as important as basketball was to me, my life went beyond the game. It was like my mother told me: when I started listening, I began to understand what my life was about. It was about God's game plan, God's design. He had merely chosen basketball to teach me.

A SMALL, SHY VOICE

HENRY WINKLER

Known the world over for his role as "the Fonz," on the TV series Happy Days,
Henry Winkler now acts, produces, and directs in television and film.

For years I played one of television's most popular characters, "The Fonz"—Arthur Fonzarelli, also known as Fonzie—that super cool guy on the hit series *Happy Days*. He came on like Marlon Brando in *The Wild One* but was really a street-sweet guy with a heart of gold.

Fonzie rode a motorcycle, and when he slicked back his hair with a flick of his comb, teenagers in the audience started shrieking. Kids all around the country greeted each other with The Fonz's familiar, "Hey . . . ay . . . AY!" In fact, Fonzie became such a part of American life that the black leather jacket he wore on the show is now displayed as part of the permanent collection at the Smithsonian Institution in Washington, D.C.

Over the years, *Happy Days* and all of its characters and cast became like a real family to me. And yet, sometimes there were doubts in my mind about Fonzie. I was trained as a classical actor at Yale Drama School, and I'd always meant to be a "serious" actor performing drama, not comedy. When interviewers asked me if I felt I was "compromising myself" by playing a character like The Fonz, I'd answer that every acting job is important if it's conveying a worthwhile message, and you adapt the part to your own talents and tastes; that it took every bit of my training and skill to make the character of Fonzie come alive on the home screen; and that it was more demanding to play comedy and bring it off successfully.

I meant every word of what I said, but occasionally I, too, would wonder: was playing the character of Fonzie doing anybody any good? I'd been raised in the Jewish faith and still felt a real peace and closeness to God when I worshiped in a synagogue. Was I doing what I was really meant to do? Was I using my God-given talents in the best possible way?

I'm chairman of an annual event called the Special Arts Festival that's held at the Music Center in Los Angeles. It's sort of a Special Olympics of the arts, where children with mental and physical handicaps come to perform in their own amateur theatrics, to show their talents, and to exhibit their artwork. The walls are filled with paintings done by the boys and girls, and music rings out as they play instruments and sing songs. It's an exciting time for everyone as the kids have a chance to display what they can do and become aware of the special contributions they can make.

Children are there from all backgrounds and all walks of life; and as I walk through the crowds, I do a lot of hugging. I hold the hand of a little girl in a wheelchair. I joke with a young boy without a leg.

Several years ago there was so much noise that it's amazing I heard the voice at all. "Fonzie," someone said—a small, shy voice in all the hubbub. "Fonzie!"

A little girl with large brown eyes and dark curls looked up at me. She was perhaps five years old—just staring at me. She didn't say another word. She wouldn't answer my questions. I just figured she was simply one of those shy ones that you see occasionally.

I told the little girl how glad I was to see her, then stood up and looked into the face of the woman who must have been her mother. But why were the woman's eyes shiny with tears?

The crowd closed around us and I went on.

And then one day I got a letter—from the mother of the little girl. She told me all about her daughter—I'll call her Claire. Claire was autistic. Autistic children are locked in a world of their own and rarely speak or communicate with others. For reasons doctors and psychologists still don't understand, autistic children are so totally self-absorbed that they don't seem to realize that anyone else exists at all.

In the entire five years of her life, Claire had not spoken a single word. Until she called out, "Fonzie!" Somehow the character of Fonzie had broken through to her, enabling her in that one mysterious moment to make a connection—with life.

The next year Claire was at the festival again, and I eagerly went to see her. This time her voice was firm and clear. "Hi, Fonzie," she said.

"Claire's teachers say she now has a vocabulary of over fifty words," her mother told me. "They can't believe what's happened."

Just at that moment Claire tugged at my hand. "My sister," she said, pointing out the young girl standing close to us. "Hug her too."

Sometimes we wonder if we're doing our best for God. We're not sure if we're doing what we should with the gifts he gave us. That little girl showed me that we simply have to do whatever comes our way to the best of our abilities. And trust that God will find his way to touch someone else with them.

And what is that trust called? It's called faith.

ARE YOU TOO OLD TO BELIEVE?

JULIUS LaROSA

Julius LaRosa's singing career included work with the United States Navy Band and on The Arthur Godfrey Show *before moving to RCA Records.*

y wife, Rory, and our five-year-old daughter, Maria, sat in the rear of the rehearsal hall while I ran through the song with the band for that night's performance in a Miami hotel. From time to time I left the microphone to lean over the stage and talk to the bandleader. This was the first time Maria had attended a rehearsal.

When it was over she hurried up to me. "Daddy," she asked, "how is it I can hear you so loud from way back where I was sitting with Mommy, but when you talked to the bandleader I can hardly hear you at all?"

"It's the microphone, Maria, it makes the sound louder."

"But how?" she persisted.

"Well, sound is measured by what they call decibels and . . ." Her large brown eyes were growing larger with perplexity. How do you explain decibels to a five-year-old? "I could tell you, sweetheart, but you really wouldn't understand. You will when you get a little older. Right now it's too advanced for you."

A few days later Maria and I were sitting together watching the sun set. "Daddy," Maria said, "where does the sun go at night? Does it go to sleep?"

"No, sweetheart, the earth turns and it goes around and . . . Maria, I could tell you, but it's really too advanced for you now."

"What's advanced?" She was really puzzled.

I hesitated, gathering my thoughts. "When you were born, Maria, your legs were very small; they weren't strong enough for you to walk. Walking was too advanced for you. But when your legs grew bigger and stronger, walking wasn't too advanced for you and you walked."

The puzzled look was fading from her face. "And when you were very small," I went on, "you couldn't eat a hot dog because you didn't have teeth yet. Hot dogs were too advanced for you until you had teeth. When something is too advanced it means you might not understand it now, but you will at the right time. Do you understand that, Maria?"

"Mmmm . . . I think so. Thanks."

Fours years after that question, I was taking Maria to church one Sunday. Her mother was going through the final stages of a pregnancy that kept her in bed. My wife was the churchgoer, I wasn't. I had stopped regular attendance after a storm of doubt.

As we approached the church, Maria asked, "How come you don't go to church anymore, Daddy?"

"I used to go, sweetheart, but one Sunday I was sitting in church and I felt like I didn't mean it anymore and I thought it would be more honest if I didn't go."

"But, Daddy, you believe what happens there. You do believe in God?" Then, hesitantly, "Don't you?"

"I don't know, Maria."

She looked up into my eyes thoughtfully—as if she were searching her mind, trying to decipher my confused answer.

"Do you think," she finally offered, "maybe it's too advanced for you?"

Inside the church her question began gnawing at me. It gnawed at me for weeks afterward, not without pain. Wiser heads than mine have yet to explain electricity or coincidence or the cosmos.

In time, all the things that made me feel "I didn't mean it anymore" seemed to answer themselves. Now, when I grope for the meaning of a sad or tragic event—a friend's child dies, an elderly relative loses a lifetime job, a plane crashes—whenever I think of all the ills that flesh is heir to, I'm reminded of the innocent wisdom of Maria, who believes in belief. And I know there are many, many things that are too advanced for me, as there are for all of us.

And I believe, I believe.

HOW TO BE AN ESKIMO

MARIETTE HARTLEY
AS TOLD TO RICHARD H. SCHNEIDER

In addition to numerous television and film roles, Mariette Hartley is perhaps best known for a series of Polaroid camera commercials she appeared in with James Garner.

Years ago in a group therapy session, I heard a story that I have never forgotten. It enlightened me about how a higher power works in our lives. It went like this:

"Hey, Father," said a man talking to a priest. "You got it all wrong about this God stuff. He doesn't exist. I oughta know."

"Why's that, my son?"

"Well, when I was ice-fishing in the Arctic far from the nearest village, a blizzard blew up with wind and blinding snow. I was a goner. So I got down on my knees and prayed real hard, begging God for help."

"And did He help you?"

"Heck no. God didn't lift a finger. Some Eskimo appeared out of nowhere and showed me the way."

It took me a while to recognize the Eskimos in my life. And I had needed them so desperately.

I grew up haunted by the teachings of my maternal grandfather, John B. Watson, a famous psychologist who founded a movement called behaviorism. It taught parents to resist their children's natural bonding needs, which he considered undesirable. There was to be no cuddling, no kissing, and few outward signs of affection. As a result of this kind of treatment as a child, my mother later learned to use alcohol to numb her feelings of isolation. And my father, a high-powered advertising executive, also succumbed to alcohol. Despite their affliction, they loved me deeply. I grew up with my younger brother in affluent Weston, Connecticut, where I discovered my calling. At eleven I joined the Silver Nutmeg Theatre Company with roles in plays like *Alice in Wonderland* and *Little Women* in elementary schools around the state.

Smitten by the theater, I met one of my first Eskimos, Eva Le Gallienne, the legendary actress, who was teaching at the White Barn Theatre nearby. Miss Le G. was a small, delightful woman with a tiny nose, violet eyes, and translucent skin. She wore lavender cashmere sweaters and periwinkle-blue dresses. A loving, giving person, she taught youngsters like me as well as professionals. I learned so much from her—how to feel and project emotions, and to let "the sacred fire strike" by eliminating self so that the character one is playing shines through.

Miss Le G. also inspired me spiritually. Though Mom and Dad were not religious, I was attracted to church. Sunday mornings I'd hop on my bicycle and pedal to the Norfield Congregational Church, where I sang solos in the choir. My early days in a dysfunctional family were traumatic, to be sure, but it was in church that I was reminded of hope and goodness.

The power and abundance of that hope became very clear to me one beautiful summer afternoon when I was sixteen and just back from a rehearsal at a nearby Shakespeare festival. I was walking in a field, and as I stopped by a tree I suddenly had an overwhelming spiritual experience. In a family of atheists, it was hard to share these feelings, and I was lucky enough to be able to tell Miss Le G. in a letter. She wrote back from London that she, too, had had a similar experience, that there were "times, alas, when I felt so utterly undeserving that I was filled with a kind of wondering humbleness, not just humility, but the sort of thing that flings you to your knees. Try terribly hard not to fail it," she continued, "always be yourself . . . never get conceited or spoiled . . . keep brave, keep strong, do the job at hand to the best of your ability . . . know that you are being used by some greater power and try to obey it."

It was my belief in a spiritual life that sustained me through the difficult years to come. As a teenager I suffered a short-lived marriage to an older man who beat me mercilessly. Later I was offered a leading role in the film *Come Fly With Me*, but a doctor misdiagnosed my hepatitis. Without proper treatment, I got too sick to take the role.

Then, most devastating of all, was my father's suicide. It happened after Dad, tormented by alcohol, had lost job after job and succumbed to hopelessness. Mother and I were eating lunch when a gunshot rang out from the bedroom. We dashed in to find he had shot himself in the head. For a year I kept hearing that gunshot and was barely able to work at all.

Finally, after fighting my own alcoholism, I went into therapy. I realized I had been skipping from one "answer" to another—acting, not acting, overeating, starving myself. And by grace I found a support group where I learned to admit my own faults and my own responsibility. I surrendered my defects to a power greater than I. Only then was I able to embrace my past, make peace with it.

Gradually I emerged from my self-imposed exile. I started accepting offers to do commercials (which I had sworn I would never do as a "serious" actress). I really started living by the belief that "When you let go of the things you think you should be doing, what you need to be doing comes to you." This was what happened to me when I appeared with James Garner in commercials for Polaroid. I played the wife, and the instant we started working together there was electricity.

The TV audience loved it and we shot almost 250 spots. Eventually, I had to wear a T-shirt proclaiming: "I am *not* Mrs. James Garner."

In 1974, I met another Eskimo, Patrick Boyriven, who became my husband. We have two children, Justine and Sean. I even discovered I had been an Eskimo myself, albeit unwittingly. It happened when Linda Hunt, the Academy Award-winning actress, rushed up to me at a premiere and said: "Oh, thank you! It's because of *you* I'm in the theater."

It turned out she had watched me, at age twelve, play Jo in the Nutmeg production of *Little Women* that toured Connecticut schools. She said she had never forgotten watching someone her own age act and love it so much.

What continually impresses me is the effect people have on one another. This was brought home to me in May 1991 when my family and I drove east to visit an Eskimo named Dolores Hart, an actress with a beautiful spirit whom I had known when she appeared in *Come Fly With Me*, the film I had missed so many years before.

Now she was Mother Dolores, a cloistered nun at an abbey in Connecticut. When I saw her—for the first time in thirty years—there was peace and wisdom in her kind eyes. She told me what she had learned from her years of contemplation in one sentence: "The only way to heal is to speak."

That is why I now speak all over the country. And I pass on Mother Dolores's message, telling people we all walk around wounded, but we can heal our wounds by helping others.

And when we get down on our knees, answers come, often in the form of Eskimos.

READY? SET! NOW!

CHRIS EVERT

Chris Evert won Wimbledon three times, the U.S. Open six times,
and the French singles championship seven times.

The court was still wet from an early morning drizzle as Tracy Austin and I began warming up for our semifinal match in the 1980 U.S. Open tennis tournament. I was worried and nervous. Not only was Tracy the top seed in the tournament, but she had beaten me the last five times we had played each other. And as I tentatively returned one of Tracy's slashing backhands, I didn't feel any confidence that today would be different.

Earlier that spring, after a grueling series of matches, I'd taken some time off from the tennis circuit. But when I resumed playing, even though I won some tournaments, I didn't feel at all like the same player who'd been number one in the world for five of the previous eight years. I'd lost the confidence I needed to play boldly and make the snap decisions so necessary in athletics. Instead, I was continually replaying the past. Poor shots would often trigger memories of past matches, where I'd made wrong decisions in similar situations. And that would make my play even worse.

By the fourth game of the first set, all my worst fears had materialized. Tracy was ahead, 4-0, and I was playing terribly.

Suddenly a loud voice boomed, "The match is starting now!" I whirled around and saw my good friend Ron Samuels standing next to his wife, television actress Lynda Carter. He was cupping one hand around his mouth—and shaking his fist at me! It made me smile—I knew Ron wasn't mad at me. It was his way of reminding me what had pulled me out of the doldrums months before, when I'd rejoined the tennis circuit. "If you decide things are going to be different," he had said, "you've made a new beginning. You don't have to worry about the past anymore." And that's what he was saying now with his clenched fist. So what if you're down 0-4. You can still turn things around. Now is the beginning!

Ron's words seemed to spur me on. I broke Tracy's serve in the next game, and even when she won the first set with a brilliant cross-court forehand, I felt my lost confidence surging. I came back to win that match, 4-6, 6-1, 6-1, and went on to win the tournament.

That U.S. Open match really did turn my tennis game around—I won fifty-nine of my last sixty-two matches that year—but it taught me an important lesson too. You don't need to let the disappointments and defeats of the past get in the way of what you're doing now. Now isn't then. Now is the beginning.

DARING TO DREAM BIG!

DIANE SAWYER

Diane Sawyer has anchored a number of high-profile television shows, including CBS This Morning, Primetime Live, *and* Good Morning America.

Many of us, I think, can look back and recall certain specific moments in our lives that take on greater importance the longer we live. "The past has a different pattern," T. S. Eliot wrote, when viewed from each of our changing perspectives.

For me, one of those moments occurred when I was seventeen years old. I was a high school senior in Louisville, Kentucky, representing my state in the 1963 America's Junior Miss competition in Mobile, Alabama. Along with the other young contestants, I was doing my best to hold up under the grueling week-long schedule of interviews, agonies over hair that curled or wouldn't, photo sessions, nervous jitters and rehearsals. In the midst of it all, there was one person who stood at the center—at least my psychological center—someone I viewed as an island in an ocean of anxiety.

She was one of the judges. A well-known writer. A woman whose sea-gray eyes fixed on you with laser penetration, whose words were always deliberate. She felt the right words could make all the difference. Her name was Catherine Marshall.

From the first moment I met Catherine Marshall, I was aware that she was holding me—indeed all of us—to a more exacting standard. While other pageant judges asked questions about favorite hobbies and social pitfalls, she sought to challenge. She felt even seventeen-year-old girls—perhaps especially seventeen-year-old girls—should be made to examine their ambitions and relate them to their values.

During the rehearsal on the last day of the pageant, the afternoon before it would all end, several of us were waiting backstage when a pageant official said Catherine Marshall wanted to speak with us. We gathered around. Most of us were expecting a last-minute pep talk or the ritual good luck wish, or at most an exhortation to be good citizens, but we were surprised.

She fixed her eyes upon us. "You have set goals for yourselves. I have heard some of them. But I don't think you have set them high enough. You have talent and intelligence and a chance. I think you should take those goals and expand them. Think of the most you could do with your lives. Make what you do matter. Above all, dream big."

It was not so much an instruction as a dare. I felt stunned, like a small animal fixed on bright lights. This woman I admired so much was disappointed in us—not by what we were but by how little we aspired to be.

I won the America's Junior Miss contest that year. In the fall I entered Wellesley College, where my sister, Linda, was beginning her junior year. I graduated in 1967 with a B.A. degree in English and a complete lack of inspiration about what I should do with it.

I went to my father, a lawyer and later a judge in Louisville's Jefferson County Court. "But what is it that you enjoy doing most?" he asked.

"Writing," I replied slowly. "I like the power of the word. And working with people. And being in touch with what's happening in the world."

He thought for a moment. "Did you ever consider television?"

I hadn't.

At that time there were few, if any, women journalists on television in our part of the country. The idea of being a pioneer in the field sounded like dreaming big. So that's how I came to get up my nerve, put on my very best Mary Tyler Moore girl journalist outfit, and go out to convince the news director at Louisville's WLKY-TV to let me have a chance.

He gave it to me—and for the next two-and-a-half years, I worked as a combination weather and news reporter.

Eventually, though, I began to feel restless. I'd lie awake at night feeling that something wasn't right. I'd wait for the revelation, the sign pointing in the direction of the Big Dream. What I didn't realize is what Catherine Marshall undoubtedly knew all along—that the dream is not the destination but the journey.

I was still working at WLKY when, in 1969, my father was killed in an auto crash. His death—coupled with my urge to make a change—spurred me in the search for a different job, and also seemed to kindle my interest in the world of government, law and politics. I racked my brain. I put out feelers. And then one of my father's associates said, "What about Washington?"

Several months later, in the autumn of 1970, I said good-bye to my mother and Linda and to the good folks at WLKY, and boarded a plane for Washington, D.C.

Now, I know this may sound incredibly naive, but when the plane landed at National Airport, I got off with a very firm idea of where I wanted to work. At the White House. True, in the eyes of official Washington I might be right off the equivalent of the turnip truck, but working in the White House was exactly what I had in mind!

Thanks to a few kind words of recommendation from a friend of my father's, I was able to obtain an interview with Ron Ziegler, the White House press secretary, and I was hired.

Those were heady days. The Press Office, located in the West Wing of the White House, was the hub for information flowing between the White House and the media. I worked hard and I worked long and loved every part of it.

Then came Watergate.

In the summer of 1974 the President resigned. Immediately I was appointed to his transition team in San Clemente, California.

My assignment on the West Coast was supposed to last only six months. But a few days after my arrival the President made a request that I was totally unprepared for. He asked me to consider staying on in San Clemente—along with several other writers and aides—to assist him in researching and writing his memoirs. I had to make a choice, and a choice that I knew would have consequences.

"Career suicide," mumbled some of my friends.

But I had worked for this man and he had been good to me. Now he was asking me for something that I was in a position to give. I have never regretted the decision. I stayed.

One day in the long exile, Catherine Marshall and her husband, Leonard LeSourd, called to say they were nearby. They came for a visit, and once again I felt the searching gaze and, implicit in it, the words, "What is next?" Again I came to appreciate the immense power of someone who is unafraid to hold other people to a standard. And again I realized the way a single uncompromising question can force reexamination of a life.

After three years as co-anchor on the CBS *Morning News*, I became co-editor of CBS's *60 Minutes* television newsmagazine. We worked at a breakneck pace with long hours and constant travel thrown in. I kept a suitcase packed at all times so that I could be ready to fly out on assignment at a moment's notice.

When I go out into the world again—and who knows where I'll be flying next?—I can almost hear a wonderful woman prodding me with her fiery challenge to stretch further and, no matter how big the dream, to dream a little bigger still. God, she seems to be saying, can forgive failure, but not failure to try.

The Power of Prayer

GRACE BEFORE GREATNESS

MARIAN ANDERSON

*In 1955, Marian Anderson became the first African American singer
to perform at New York City's Metropolitan Opera.*

Failure and frustration are in the unwritten pages of everyone's record. I
have had my share of them. If my mother's gentle hands had not been there
to guide me, perhaps my life in music would have ended long ago.

The faith my mother taught me is my foundation. It is the only ground on
which I stand; with it I have a freedom in life I could not have in any other way.
Whatever is in my voice, my faith has put it there. The particular religion a child
echoes is an accident of birth, but I was converted to my mother's faith and patient
understanding long before I could define either.

We were poor. But there was a wealth in our poverty, a wealth of music and love
and faith. My two sisters, Alice and Ethel, and I were all in the junior church choir.
I still have a vivid memory of our mother and father, their faces shining with pride,
watching us from the front pews. And once when I was six, I was fortunate enough
to be selected to step out in front of the choir and sing "The Lord Is My Shepherd."

It was a Baptist church we attended in Philadelphia. But my mother taught us
early that the form of one's faith is less important than what is in one's heart.

"When you come to him," she said, "he never asks what you are."

We children never heard her complain about her lot or criticize those who
offended her. One of her guiding precepts has always been: "Never abuse those who
abuse you. Bear them no malice, and theirs will disappear."

My sisters still attend that Baptist church in Philadelphia. It is a church and a congregation I hold most fondly in my heart for many reasons. These were the people who, years ago, pooled their pennies into what they grandly called "The Fund for Marian Anderson's Future," a gesture of love and confidence impossible to forget in a lifetime. When I returned to Philadelphia, I always tried to see some of these people who had been so important to me, and, though it seldom is possible these days, I love to sing in their choir.

My father died when I was twelve, and my mother's burden became heavier. Before she became a housewife and the mother of three daughters, she was a schoolteacher. Now she became a father to us as well as a mother, and earned our whole livelihood by taking in washing. It was terribly difficult for her, I know, but she would not even hear of any of us children leaving school for work.

During those years I began to have my first opportunities to earn a little money by singing. Almost entirely, they were Sunday evening concerts for the church, or for the YWCA and the YMCA. At these affairs I could sing, perhaps two or three songs, and my fee was a very grand fifty cents or, once in a great while, one dollar. Sometimes I would dash to four or five of these concerts in one evening.

Many people were kind to me: teachers who took no fees and those who urged me forward when I was discouraged. Gradually I began to sing with glee clubs and churches in other cities. After one minor effort in Harlem, I was hastily sponsored for a concert in Town Hall in New York by a group of well-meaning people.

It seemed at once incredible and wonderful. But I wasn't ready. Indeed, I was far from it, both in experience and maturity. On the exciting night of my first real concert I was told Town Hall was sold out. While waiting in a dazed delight to go on, my sponsor said there would be a slight delay. I waited five, ten, fifteen minutes. Then peeked through the curtain.

The house was half empty! I died inside. But when the curtain went up I sang my heart out. And when the concert was over, I knew I had failed. The critics next day agreed with me, but what they said was really not so important. I was shattered because, inside, I felt I had let down all those people who had had faith and confidence in me. It seemed irrevocable.

"I'd better forget all about singing and do something else," I told my mother.

"Why don't you think about it a little and pray a lot, first?" she cautioned.

She had taught me to make my own decisions when I could, and pray for the right ones when I could not. But I did not heed her now. I refused a few offers to sing at other concerts. I avoided my music teacher. For a whole year I brooded in silence. My mother suffered because I was not expressing myself in the only way that brought me happiness. But she knew I had to find my own way back. From time to time she just prodded me gently: "Have you prayed, Marian? Have you prayed?"

No, I hadn't. Nothing would help. I embraced my grief. It was sufficient. But in those tearful hours there slowly came the thought that there is a time when even the most self-sufficient cannot find enough strength to stand alone. Then, one prays with a fervor one never had before. From my torment I prayed with the sure knowledge there was someone to whom I could pour out the greatest need of my heart and soul. It did not matter if he answered. It was enough to pray.

Slowly I came out of my despair. My mind began to clear. No one was to blame for my failure. Self-pity left me. In a burst of exuberance I told my mother, "I want to study again. I want to be the best, be loved by everyone, and be perfect in everything."

"That's a wonderful goal," she chided. "But our dear Lord walked this earth as the most perfect of all beings, yet not everybody loved him."

Subdued, I decided to return to my music and to seek humility before perfection.

One day I came home from my teacher unaware that I was humming. It was the first music I had made at home in a whole year. My mother heard it and she rushed to meet me. She put her arms around me and kissed me. It was her way of saying, "Your prayers have been answered, and mine have too."

For a brief moment we stood there silently. Then my mother defined the sweet spell of our gratitude, "Prayer begins where human capacity ends," she said.

The golden echo of that moment has always been with me through the years of struggle that followed. I have been blessed with an active career and the worldly goods that come with it. If sometimes I do not hear the echo of that moment but listen only to the applause, my mother reminds me quickly of what should come first, "Grace must always come before greatness."

PANIC

AL KASHA

*Al Kasha was a successful singer, songwriter, and record producer
when he was stricken with agoraphobia and the resulting panic attacks.*

Our bags had already been checked on board. My wife and I were just about to enter the plane to fly from Los Angeles to New York for a vacation. Then the flight attendant asked to see our boarding passes.

Terror swept through me. I felt nauseous. "I—I can't do it!" I said. I turned to my wife, Ceil. "I can't go on the flight."

Ceil tried to calm me down. "Come on, Al," she said. "You can do it. I'll be right next to you. Just *try* to get on. You can listen to the music or watch the movie. It won't last very long. It'll be over in no time."

Instead of calming down I began to panic. "No! No!" I exclaimed. "I just can't do it! I'm sorry, but I can't." We drove back home to Beverly Hills. Our luggage arrived safely in New York.

How had this happened to me—an American success story? From childhood in a small, cluttered apartment in Brooklyn, I had become a successful songwriter, record producer, and writer of movie themes. With my partner, Joel Hirschhorn, I had won two Oscars. Now everything seemed to be coming apart. I was unable to get on a plane, go into a store, or even leave the house without being gripped by a paralyzing fear. There's a medical name for this. It's called agoraphobia. But then I had no idea what was happening and even less of an idea that I wasn't alone.

Ironically, some of the very things that had pushed me to succeed were now pulling me down. In the beginning I'd thrived on competition, and much of that competitiveness was born in my own family. I had always felt a driving need to please my parents; and I'd come to look upon my older brother, Larry, who had become a Broadway producer, as a rival. Each successful song I wrote made it necessary to write another. Instead of giving me satisfaction, all my achievements only made me press on.

The first attack occurred at a most unexpected time.

The day after Joel and I won our first Oscar for the song "The Morning After," my mother called to congratulate me. "An Oscar is fine," she said, "but when you win a Tony on Broadway, like your brother, then you really have made it."

Those words caused a startling reaction in me. Standing there, holding the phone, I felt my heart begin to pound so hard that I could barely breathe. My palms were drenched and my legs buckled under me. I felt as if I were going to faint, as though I were going to die. The attack didn't last long, but it bewildered me. And frightened me. I didn't want to mention it to anyone, even Ceil.

Before long, however, I began to experience moments when fear would take over without warning. Soon I was unable to drive on a freeway without hyperventilating. The first time this happened, Ceil and I were taking our six-year-old daughter, Dana, to Disneyland. I pulled over and grabbed for the door, desperate to escape the confinement of the car. I asked Ceil to drive and told her to go back home.

A few weeks later Joel and I were having lunch in a restaurant. Just as our sandwiches were arriving, I stood up and said, "We've got to leave!" Joel tried to calm me down, but I tore outside. Even though I tried, I couldn't enter another restaurant for two years.

My world kept narrowing. Panic swept over me at the thought of going into a supermarket, even the one right across the street from my house. Once, I made the effort to go, only to leave all my packages in the cart in the middle of the aisle. Eventually I couldn't even step outside the front door. I spent all my time in my study.

I began to turn down work because it was impossible for me to have meetings in anyone's office. I rejected an offer to score a film in England, and persuaded the stars of a Broadway musical Joel and I were writing to come to my home to rehearse the songs.

Joel made excuses for me each time I ducked out of an appointment, telling people I was "under the weather." My work as a freelance songwriter made it possible for me to cover up my phobias, but I was in constant fear that my secret would come out.

One of the worst things about my panic attacks was that I didn't know what was causing them. I went to several analysts, but they seemed as puzzled as I was. It was only three years after my first attack when I heard the word *agoraphobia* on a television program.

Shortly afterward, I saw a behavioral therapist who was willing to come to my home. She confirmed that I was indeed a victim of agoraphobia (fear of open or public places), the paralyzing anxiety brought on by tension and repressed hostility. She said I wasn't alone: The National Institute of Mental Health estimates that one adult in every twenty suffers from it.

I began attending group therapy sessions, but the meetings only frustrated me when I was unable to overcome my fears. I started taking tranquilizers. Home life became an endless series of fights as Ceil grew unable to understand why I couldn't cope, and my anger increased at her inability to help me.

Finally one night Ceil had had enough. She packed my bag and told me to leave. "You've stopped going to the meetings," she cried. "You won't go to a psychiatrist. You won't help yourself, so how can I help you?"

I was hurt and angry. "Nobody can help me," I snapped then left.

I spent the next three weeks in a friend's apartment. One night I was still awake at three in the morning. Instead of taking a tranquilizer, I picked up the remote control for the television and pushed the button. I could hear the set in the next room come on.

A rerun of a Robert Schuller program was being broadcast. As I lay sprawled out on the bed, I heard Dr. Schuller say, "Love casts out all fear."

My heart started to pound. My hands grew sweaty. How ironic, I thought. With me it's the opposite—fear casts out all love.

Then Dr. Schuller said, "Only Jesus Christ can set you free from your bondage." I was soaked with sweat and felt a tremendous pressure on my chest. Once more I was afraid—of dying, of losing control. Whatever happened, I had to be in control. Nobody could help me, not even God.

Or could he?

Without knowing why, I slid out of bed and crawled on hands and knees into the next room. "Jesus," I cried as I approached the television set. I saw a tremendous light streaming in through the side window. Then a voice said, "You are My son, and I love you."

It was as if God Himself were talking to me, telling me, "I love you just as you are. You don't have to prove yourself to Me. All I want is for you to trust Me, and let Me take over."

I blacked out. When I woke up almost three hours later, the television was still on. I got up and shut it off. Intuitively I sensed that something was different in me. As I moved through the apartment I realized my shoulders were taller, my step was lighter. Something was missing, and I laughed when I discovered what it was. That constant weight of having to be in control, of being on top of things, was gone. In its place was peace. For the first time in a long time, I felt at peace.

Yet even though the need for control was gone—what about the fear?

I wanted to see my wife and daughter. I had swung out the front door and gotten into the car before it hit me—I was outside! I didn't need to call Ceil and ask her to pick me up; I could drive to see her all by myself. I opened the glove compartment. The Valium tablets were there, but I didn't need them.

By the time I got to the house, I was shaking—but with laughter, not fear. I ran up to the door, rang the bell, and grabbed a very startled Ceil Kasha.

"I'm home!" I shouted. "I love you, honey!"

Poor Ceil didn't know whether to laugh or cry. She wasn't sure whether I was cured or had cracked up altogether!

Turning my life over to Christ didn't immediately solve my problems. It took months of hard work and help from family and friends to conquer the symptoms of agoraphobia, and to deal with its root causes. My greatest help came from knowing that God loved me and was with me. I didn't need to fight the battle on my own. Philippians 4:13 became one of my favorite Bible verses: "I can do all things through Christ which strengtheneth me" (KJV).

It had taken me forty-one years of life to finally find God—or to let Him find me—on October 8, 1978. Since that night, I have gone back to writing songs with Joel, and I have started an organization called "Faith over Fear" to help other agoraphobia victims. If you are one, I want you to know that you are not alone—in one week I received over eighteen hundred pieces of mail from other sufferers.

For those people who saw me accepting the Oscar in 1973 and thought, that guy has everything, my answer is, "Yes, I had everything—but it was really nothing without God."

THE POWER OF PRAYER

ED SULLIVAN

As host of a television variety show that ran from 1948 to 1971, Ed Sullivan introduced future stars such as The Beatles and Elvis Presley to the American public.

hen I was eighteen, I was a twelve-dollars-a-week sports editor of the Port Chester, New York, *Daily Item*. When the *Hartford Post* offered me a fifty-dollars-a-week job, there was a farewell banquet and speeches—glowing speeches about the bright future in Hartford.

Four days after I started work with the *Hartford Post*, the owner announced he was selling the paper. All employees would be given two weeks' pay.

My whole world crashed. How could I go back to Port Chester? My successor at the *Item* was already at work. At eighteen, a lot of false pride can confuse your thinking. And at eighteen every setback is a major calamity.

I got a job in a Hartford department store, wrapping bundles. Everybody in Connecticut was buying pots and pans that week. And wrapping paper neatly around the handles of pans requires artistry not possessed by an ex-sportswriter.

Then an infection developed on the right side of my lower jaw. The pain became so bad I couldn't sleep. I was alone, too proud to go home, in pain, and discouraged.

Just a few years before, as a student at St. Mary's School in Port Chester, I would recite the Rosary, rattling off the responses so rapidly that it became singsong, devoid of meaning. But when you're in trouble and kneel in prayer by your bed, the "Hail Mary" becomes a very personal salutation. And your plea: "Pray for us sinners" is the complete recognition of your helplessness—and your faith.

Every young man comes to one crossroad where he is tested for manhood. At this point in Hartford, prayer helped me grow up. I quit feeling sorry for myself, stuck in a job I didn't like, and went on my own to the Hartford Hospital Clinic, where a young, cheerful doctor cleaned out the infection in my jaw.

Several days later I returned from the department store to find a letter for me on the hallway table. The upper left-hand corner had the imprint, *New York Evening Mail*. I tore it open. It was from Sam Murphy, Sports Editor of the *Mail* and one of my job contacts.

"Dear Sullivan," he wrote. "I have recommended you to our school-page editor, Jack Jacowitz, to cover sports for him. Can you be in New York Monday morning?"

Could I! I wrapped my last pot and pan that Saturday night, caught an express train to Port Chester and home. That same night I was proudly showing to my mother, father, three sisters, and brother that letter and its offer of a job on a big New York daily.

On Monday morning, I went to work on the *Mail* and, for weeks afterward, was staring openmouthed at all the big-name newspaper writers along Park Row.

All of my life I've been blessed, first with a wonderful father and mother, sisters and brothers; later with an exceptional wife, special daughter, and splendid son-in-law. My TV show dropped into my lap by complete accident. It is my deepest belief that all of these things have resulted from prayer—not so much my own—but prayers of priests and nuns I have known and with whom I've been privileged to work.

So I know about the power of prayer. I know it keeps you steady, unshaken, and able to take pain. I know it will guide you to your place—the place that will best help you grow.

THE SECRET RUDOLPH VALENTINO TAUGHT ME

DAGMAR GODOWSKY

Dagmar Godowsky appeared in numerous silent films
in Hollywood during the 1920s.

The other night I watched a revival of a Rudolph Valentino movie, and I sat there with tears in my eyes through the whole film. Valentino is remembered mostly as a great ladies' man; but one day, many years ago, I saw a side of him that few people knew existed, and the experience changed my life.

I became stage-struck at an early age, and with it came a case of excruciating stage fright. When I was to perform, I would grow increasingly colder as curtain time neared, and I'd be sure I couldn't go on.

Once on stage, however, I always regained my composure and could proceed through the performance without any problems. Even though I knew my fears were temporary, I could never avoid them and I always dreaded going to the theater for the nightly suffering.

In making movies, my fears were worse. The "takes" were short, and there was always much waiting around as the camera crew and the light crew rearranged their equipment. For me, those waiting periods were like waiting for the curtain to go up, and I spent most of the day in a state of absolute terror.

In 1924, I was cast in the title role of *A Sainted Devil*, playing opposite Rudolph Valentino. The picture was being made at the Famous Players-Lasky Studio on Long

Island. The morning I headed for the studio for the first day's work, I could feel the fears and the nausea rising inside me; and by the time I walked on to the set, I was actually ill. And I went on like that, day after day.

Making matters worse was the fact that we had to shoot many of the scenes twice, for the American and European versions. This meant the picture would take longer to make than usual, and I was sure I would never survive.

This time, the fright was greater than ever before. I wondered if working with a superstar like Valentino was the reason. But I had worked with superstars before— Lionel Barrymore, Wallace Reid, Alla Nazimova. I couldn't understand my panic, and I thought seriously of giving up acting if it were going to keep having this effect on me.

We had been working on *A Sainted Devil* for a month when, at the end of a day, Valentino came to my dressing room and asked, "Daggie, did you bring your car to the studio today?"

"I don't have a car, Rudy. I don't like to drive. I use taxis," I replied.

"Then let me give you a lift into town," he said. "I want to talk to you about something."

Minutes later, Valentino was driving us into the city, and we chatted idly about nothing special. I wondered what was on his mind and when we would get to it. We entered Manhattan on the Fifty-ninth Street Bridge and, after a few blocks, Rudy drew the car up to a curb and parked.

"I make this stop twice a day, going to work and coming back. Let's go in," Rudy said.

I looked at the building. It was a Catholic church. Although I am not a Catholic, I had been educated in Catholic convents in Europe, so I knew how I should act. We went into the church, Rudy chose a pew, we genuflected together, then entered the pew and knelt. From the movement of his lips, I could tell that Rudy was praying. Since he was Italian, I had assumed he was a Catholic, but I had no idea that he was devout.

Then he startled me by turning to me suddenly and saying, "Daggie, I'm worried about you. We all are. Why do you always seem to be on your deathbed all day? What's wrong?"

Frustrated, I said, "I don't know, Rudy. I have been like this ever since I started acting. I'm all right once I get going, but it kills me to get started. I am always so afraid."

"I used to be like that," he said.

I couldn't believe it. "You were?"

He nodded. "Yes. You at least attended acting school before you went to work. I didn't. I fell into this business because a few of the right people thought I photographed well. At first I was terrified that the other actors—the directors, the crews—would see how lousy I was, and I got sick as a dog every day."

"How did you get over it?"

He pointed at the altar, then said, "I decided that God was my only audience. I decided that if I had any acting ability, it was because he gave it to me. God became the only one I had to satisfy. Since then, every morning on the way to work I stop off in a church and ask God for a good day. Going home, I stop off again, thanking him or asking him why the day had gone badly. He's always told me."

"How?" I asked.

"He tells my heart," Rudy said, "usually by reminding me that my troubles are my own because I have been unkind or thoughtless or shortsighted. I ask Him to help me change. Anyway, in time I lost my fears about what others thought of me and cared only about what God thought of me, not only as an actor but as a man. And I stopped getting sick."

"I wish I could," I said.

"You can," he said, "and I will help you. As long as we are working on this movie, I'm going to pick you up every morning and we are going to make a stop here. And we will stop off again on our way back. Daggie, you've got to learn to trust God before you can know how to love him. And once you love him, he will take care of all your problems."

Going to work the next morning, Valentino and I stopped at the church, and I asked God for a good day. On the set, as we were awaiting the day's first take, Rudy said, "Now, Daggie, remember who your audience is." I kept remembering all day. That evening in the church, I was able to thank God for the least troubled day of my career. Gradually I learned that all aspects of my life became less troubled as long as I kept remembering that I had an unseen audience who was always watching over me, and that brought me an inner peace that has lasted over the years.

People tell me that I must have many wonderful memories about the golden era of the silent movies. I do, and my favorite memory is that the screen's greatest lover taught me how to love God.

THE VOW I ALMOST FORGOT

DANNY THOMAS

While a well-known actor, Danny Thomas's lasting legacy is St. Jude's Research
Hospital, an insitution dedicated to finding cures for catastrophic childhood diseases.

Many people seem to know that I once vowed to Saint Jude that I'd build a shrine in his name if he'd help me through a difficult time in my life. Yet the fascinating part of that story is how, when I failed to keep my part of the bargain, that saint resolutely refused to let me off the hook.

If you're not a Catholic, as I am, such talk of shrines and vows and saints might sound a bit strange, but when I was growing up in a deeply religious family in Toledo, Ohio, these things were familiar matters. My parents had come from Lebanon, a country where shrines dedicated to favorite patron saints are familiar sights. Often these shrines are simply statues, or little places where you can stop to meditate and pray.

We Catholics, of course, do not worship these patron saints—we worship only God—but we do look upon them as special intercessors with God; and we choose them as our guardians and protectors. And, believe me, as one of nine kids in a very poor immigrant family, I was grateful for all the protection I could get!

My mother did not hesitate to make her own spiritual vows. I remember especially a solemn promise she made shortly after the birth of my youngest brother. His name was Danny. At that time my name was Amos—Amos Jacobs—but early in my show business career, I took the names of my youngest and oldest brothers and became Danny Thomas.

When the first Danny was a few months old, he was badly bitten by a rat that jumped into his crib. He screamed and went into convulsions. At the hospital the doctors told my mother that Danny was dying, but she wouldn't accept that. She went to her knees in prayer, promising God that if her baby's life were saved she'd beg alms for the poor for a year.

Danny got well; and every day for twelve months my mother, herself one of the poorest of the poor, living in shabby, cramped quarters over a pool hall, went out and begged pennies from door to door.

My mother's faith in God was so strong that she could not possibly give in to fear or hopelessness. To her, despair was a tool of the devil—it was doubting God, and that was a sin. As each of us children was born, she turned us over to God; and after that she would not let herself, or us, forget that we had Him to turn to.

When I was ten years old, I landed a job hawking soda pop in the old Columbia burlesque theater in Toledo, which meant that I wouldn't get home until 2:30 in the morning. One day I heard a neighbor asking my mother if she was worried about the things that might happen to her little boy, but my mother's reply rang with certainty. "Amos is safe," she said. "I've given him into the care of the Blessed Mother." She knew that I was in good hands, and so did I.

I always had my heart set on being an entertainer; and during the seven years I spent at the burlesque theater; I studied some of the best comedians in the business and grew all the more determined to be one too. I quit school at sixteen and worked as a busboy, a night watchman, a drill-press operator's assistant, all the while picking up odd jobs singing and clowning at local banquets. Eventually I went to Detroit and sang for a while on a radio program. That's where I met and married Rosemarie, who's been my wife ever since. And that's where I faced the first real crisis of my life.

In June 1940, a baby was on the way. I was making two dollars a night as an emcee at a Detroit supper club called the Club Morocco. Then it was announced that on Saturday night the club would close for good. I had no job and no prospects.

Rosemarie was urging me to consider looking for a more reliable line of work, but all I wanted was show business. I wasn't worried about our future. I wasn't in despair—my mother had taught me too well for that—but the time had come when I had to choose a realistic career to provide for my family.

Rosemarie talked about my going into the grocery business. I had to consider her wishes. Maybe she was right; maybe I could never make my way—and ours—as an entertainer. I was in agony of indecision.

On Tuesday night a man came into the Club Morocco. He was celebrating something. His pockets were filled with little cards that he was handing out to people as he tried to tell them about an incredible thing that had just happened to him. His wife was in a hospital where she'd been facing an operation for a deadly cancer. All night long this man had knelt on the cold marble floor of the hospital and prayed the same prayer over and over again. When the sun came up in the morning, the doctors called him in to report that, inexplicably, miraculously, his wife's cancer had disappeared.

"This is the prayer that did it," he said, handing me one of the cards. It was the prayer to Saint Jude.

All that night I thought about this man and his appeal to a saint whom I knew only slightly as "Patron of the Hopeless" or "The Forgotten Saint." Though an apostle of Jesus, Jude was not one of the saints to whom many Catholics turned, probably because his name, Judas Thaddeus, was far too similar to that of the hated Judas Iscariot.

The next day I went into a church to pray; and when I reached into my pocket for a coin, I found the card the man had given me. Then and there I felt moved to make my vow. I did not ask for anything specific like money or fame; but I promised Saint Jude that if he would help me find some clear course for my life, I would build him a shrine.

The day after the Club Morocco closed, I drove my old Buick down to Toledo and left Rosemarie with my parents while I took one last stab at looking for work in show business. My plan was to go to Cleveland where I had a number of contacts, but at the last moment, I turned the other way and went to Chicago. It was almost as though I was being drawn there.

Chicago became my town. Very quickly, one little radio job led to another, and in a short time I was flourishing as a character actor. Then I tried my hand again as a stand-up entertainer. I opened before eighteen customers in a converted automobile showroom called the 5100 Club; in a few months there were that many people waiting outside trying to get in. Success simply piled upon success.

And what happened to my vow to Saint Jude? Nothing. I was so busy that, for two years, I had forgotten about it. But Saint Jude had not.

On the way home after a night out, I used to go to the 5:00 A.M. mass at Saint Clement's Church. One morning I picked up a little pamphlet that lay beside me in the pew and, to my surprise, read about a novena—a nine-day period of devotion—about to be offered to none other than my old friend Saint Jude. Even more surprising was the information that there, on the south side of Chicago, was the first national shrine to Saint Jude. Chicago was Saint Jude's town too! He wanted me to know it.

I did not forget Saint Jude again. I knew I had to do something about fulfilling my vow, but I couldn't make up my mind what kind of a shrine I should build. Rosemarie suggested that I think about a statue, or perhaps a side altar, but somehow nothing seemed right to me. Time went by. I moved on to New York. My career progressed to movies and TV. Still I could not make up my mind.

And then came the dream.

I dreamed one night about a little boy being injured in a car accident. He was rushed to the hospital, but for some reason the doctors were reluctant to treat him and the boy bled to death. The dream was so vivid, so horrifying, that it troubled me for days. But out of that dream came an idea, an idea born of a lifetime of experiences. I thought about the man who had prayed for his wife all night on the cold hospital floor. I thought of my infant brother Danny grabbing hold of life just when the doctors said he was dying, and slowly I began to see Saint Jude's shrine as a hospital. And what better way to honor the Patron Saint of the Hopeless than with a place where "dying" children, children with "incurable" diseases could come to be healed?

That, of course, was the beginning of Saint Jude's Children's Research Hospital in Memphis, Tennessee. It is the only institution on this earth dedicated solely to the conquest of catastrophic diseases. It is open to children of all faiths and races, regardless of their parents' ability to pay. No family ever pays for the services rendered there. They are free.

It took me ten years to raise the money to get the hospital started. I did it mainly through benefit performances, going all over the country raising money from Catholics and Protestants and Jews—and Muslims too—and especially getting help from people of my own Lebanese heritage. I never went before one of those benefit audiences without thinking about my mother going door-to-door begging pennies; for, in my own way, I was doing the same thing, for the same reason.

Today when I look at the hospital that Saint Jude brought into being, when I see the hope that the Saint of the Hopeless has brought to thousands of parents and their youngsters, I am as certain as my mother was certain, that to fight despair is to affirm our faith in God and in the love he has for all of us.

SOMETHING MORE

MIKE SCHMIDT

Mike Schmidt won the National League's "Most Valuable Player" award three times during his eighteen years with the Philadelphia Phillies.

The best and worst year of my life started with a telephone call. From that moment on, a whole series of strange things started in motion; I haven't been the same person since.

The call came just after baseball season ended in the fall of 1977. Andre Thornton was on the line. "How about getting together sometime?" he said. I was surprised to hear from him. Andy was the first baseman for the Cleveland Indians—a real first-class fellow. We'd been in the minors together, but now we were playing in different leagues; and I hadn't seen much of him. I did remember seeing him at batting practice one day the year before, when he'd come around the batting cage to talk to me. The unusual glow on his face that day sort of stuck in my mind.

I learned the reason for Andy's call a week later, when he and his wife, Gert, came to dinner with Donna and me at our house in Cherry Hill, New Jersey. Andy was a very religious man, something I was not, and he'd seen an item in one of the sports columns where I'd mentioned God. Well, the press is always putting words into players' mouths, and I couldn't remember having said anything about God to any reporter.

It was true that recently I had started dropping in to baseball chapel before the game on Sundays. Maybe that's how the item got in the sports column. However, the weird thing about it was that I *had* been doing some thinking that you might call "spiritual." Something was happening to me; something was making me feel uneasy. As we sat down to dinner I wondered if Andy had sensed that.

Actually, things were going so well for me in those days that it seemed silly to feel uneasy. My life had been charmed ever since college when I was all-American in baseball at Ohio University. The Phillies had drafted me in 1971, and except for a rotten rookie year, my career had been on a steady upswing. I'd been the National League's home-run leader in 1974, 1975, and 1976; and I knew I was on my way to becoming the highest-paid player in the league. Still, I couldn't forget the afternoon a few weeks back when I was outside our house casually shooting baskets in the driveway hoop. There was a moment when I looked over at the Mercedes and Corvette parked there. Out back was our swimming pool; inside the house, my beautiful Donna was busy in the kitchen. "What did I do to deserve all this?" I said to myself. "Why am I so blessed?" It was a strange thing to say, but success was bothering me.

We had a good time that night, two baseball players and our wives sharing a meal and lively talk. Gradually the conversation turned serious, and Andy brought up some of the very things that had been on *my* mind, such as why we should have been singled out for baseball stardom, and what it all meant: the prestige, the money, the sports cars, the mansions. It didn't surprise me that Andy related everything to faith in God, and I was impressed with his knowledge of the Bible, yet the memorable part of the evening was still to come. We turned to the subject of families.

Gert and Andy began telling us about their two children, little Theresa and Andy Junior. From across the table Donna and I looked at each other. We each knew what the other was thinking. "Well," I said out loud, "we talk about having it all, but there's one thing Donna and I don't have, something we've been denied—a child."

Andy Thornton was very moved by this, and right then and there, while we were still at the table, he said a prayer for us. In simple, direct, beautiful words he asked God to give Donna and me patience and understanding—and a child of our own.

The evening came to a close. Gert and Andy climbed into their van, waved good-bye, and drove away.

One week later, Gert and Andy were riding in that same van with their two children. There was a sleet storm. The van skidded and crashed. Andy and their son escaped with minor injuries. Gert and their daughter were killed.

And one week after that, Donna learned she was pregnant.

This was just the start of that best and worst year of my life. The grace with which Andy met and survived his heartbreak inspired everyone in baseball, and the public as well. It led me to think deeply about the kind of faith Andy had. I pictured again the glow I'd seen on his face the day he'd called me over by the batting cage. I remembered now how he'd told me about his having given "the reins" of his life to Christ. I thought, at the time, he'd gone off the deep end.

The winter set in. Donna was doing well. But I was still wrestling with my own uneasy thoughts about life, when I happened to come across a calling card in my wallet. It read: Dr. Wendell Kempton, President of the Association of Baptists for World Evangelism.

Kempton had been a speaker at one of those Sunday baseball chapels and he'd talked about having been a heavy drinker, "a real party animal," before his conversion. I'd been impressed by him. Now I didn't even telephone; I drove right to his office in New Jersey. When he seemed pleased to see me, I sat down and said, "Can we just talk?"

Before I left his office, Wendell suggested getting together for dinner and a short session of Bible study at his house. "Why not bring your wife along?" he said. "And any players who might want to come."

Some "short session"! What was supposed to be a half-hour Bible lesson turned into a six-hour marathon in which Wendell traced God's plan of salvation from Genesis through Revelation. We were spellbound. In awe. And so eager to hear more that we decided to meet again in ten days, this time at my house.

By then things were really churning inside me. "Am I living for the Corvette and Mercedes out there in the driveway?" I asked myself. There had to be something more.

Alone in our bedroom one day, I came across a pamphlet, a tract, with something on it called "The Sinner's Prayer." I started to read it, then I began to say the words out loud, then little by little those words became my words. I acknowledged my flaws. I acknowledged my need of Jesus. I asked him to come into my life and be my personal Savior.

At our next Bible class, which six other players and their wives attended, I told everyone what had happened. The group was stunned. Yet when I described what it was like to turn over the reins to Jesus, I think no one thought I'd gone off the deep end.

Spring came. Donna was plump and happy. Together we signed up for some natural-childbirth classes. By the time I went to spring training in Clearwater, I was feeling great. I could tell that this was going to be my best year so far.

How wrong can a guy be?

First I bruised my ribs and was on the disabled list for a month. Things went downhill from there. Out of 513 at-bats that year, I got only 129 hits. I struck out 103 times. My batting average was an anemic .251. The press got on my back. The "boo-birds" in the stands never let up. The harder I tried, the worse things got.

"What's this all about?" I asked Wendell Kempton in desperation. "I become a Christian and this is what happens?"

Wendell was patient with me. He knew that eventually I'd understand that being a Christian did not guarantee clear sailing all the time. And he counted on my remembering that I, after all, was the baseball player who had put the worship of God above "success." Meanwhile, Wendell gave me some advice that helped relieve the pressure.

"Mike," he suggested, "when you come to bat, tell the Lord outright that you're going to give him one hundred percent. If you strike out, you'll strike out doing your best. If you get a hit, that'll be doing your best too. Put the outcome in his hands."

I tried it. It was tough at first, when the "fans" were screaming for my blood and the negative thoughts crowded in. *Oh . . . I'm oh for four*, I'd think. *Fifty thousand people are expecting me to DO something.*

Then I'd pray, *Lord, clear my mind. Let Your will be done.*

It helped. It helped me get through the season, which, as it turned out, was truly the worst year in baseball I ever had.

But then it was the best year too, because of Jessica. I was there in the hospital, suited up like a doctor in a gown and mask, watching as my daughter was born. Within minutes, they placed her in my hands. I remember noticing a fleck of crimson on her tiny cheek, where the scalpel had lightly scratched her. Today Jessica is a pretty girl of nine, and that scar is so minuscule that you can see it only if you're looking for it. But it's very dear to me because it reminds me of that wonderful moment when I first held her, and everything on earth and in heaven fell into place.

In that unforgettable moment I knew for certain that life wasn't about money or status or cars, or even baseball stardom. It's about things like loving God, serving others; it's about families and husbands and wives loving and respecting one another; it's about having kids to raise and love.

Don't get me wrong; my baseball career is still very important to me. But nowadays I can get a home-run feeling just walking my kids to the school bus in the morning or playing a game of golf or hugging Donna or telling someone about Jesus.

The simple things can give you a home-run feeling too.

ATTITUDE!

CHI CHI RODRIGUEZ

Born into poverty in Puerto Rico, Chi Chi Rodriguez went on
to become one of the top ten golfers of his time.

Chi Chi's my name and golf is my game. But when I was born in Rio Pedras, Puerto Rico, my name wasn't Chi Chi. Mama and Papa named me Juan Antonio after John the Baptist and Saint Anthony. Because baseball is very big in the Caribbean and my hero was a local player named Chi Chi Flores, I ran around asking everybody to call me Chi Chi. And they did.

As for golf, I didn't know what a putter or a driver was. As a seven-year-old, all I knew was how tired I got plowing a sugarcane field behind a team of oxen all day. But it helped to put food on the table for my five brothers and sisters and me. Sometimes we ate a real dinner only twice a week. Sometimes our meal was just coffee. Even so, we kids were brought up to share what we had; and as famished as Papa might be, he'd give his last plate of beans to a hungry youngster. He was that kind of man. "Jesus asks us to be compassionate and sharing," he'd tell us, "and that gives you peace of mind." Papa had that peace, even if he worked like a horse all his life.

Little by little I began hearing of other people who didn't have to work so hard. Some of my friends talked about money to be made at a fancy place nearby called the Berwind Country Club. They played a game called golf there. The game didn't interest me then, but earning money for carrying the bags of the players sounded a lot better than following those oxen.

I knew nothing about caddying; however, Mama always taught us that when you're not sure what to do, just take the next logical step. She called this "walking in faith." And so one day I did just that: I walked down from that sun-scorched cane field into the strange new world of the Berwind Country Club.

At first I caddied just for the pay. But then the game itself started to fascinate me. I found a long piece of pipe and nailed one end of a guava limb to it. Then I invented my own game of hitting a tin can around our baseball diamond from plate to plate. Those years behind the oxen had given me forearm muscles for a vicious swing.

When not working, we caddies used to sneak onto the course; and with beat-up discarded clubs, we'd play to see who could win the most holes. Once, to my astonishment, I sank a forty-foot putt. But then the ball popped out—all by itself! I couldn't believe it. I looked again. A toad had been sitting in that hole, and when the ball rolled in, he jumped out from under it. I lost the hole. After that, when I sank a long putt, I used to run and quickly put my hat over the hole so the ball couldn't pop out.

As a teenager, I was hitting the ball pretty well, and some of the club members began to encourage me to think of golf as a career. They said if I really concentrated on it, I might be able to earn a lot of money on the PGA Tour. However, at nineteen I went into the U.S. Army. About that same time, some of my family, including my mother, left Puerto Rico and moved to New York.

On my first army leave, I went to New York, only to be dismayed by what I found. Back home I'd always thought that everybody in New York must be rich—maybe because of the way some neighbors who had moved there acted when they returned to visit. They'd put a hundred-dollar bill on top of a wad of singles and our eyes would pop. But when I saw the dismal, dirty tenement my family lived in, I told Mama, "No, you can't stay here anymore."

I went back to my army base in Oklahoma vowing to get her out of that place, *somehow*. That "somehow" turned out to be golf; waiting in the barracks was a set of clubs sent to me by one of the men I used to caddy for in Puerto Rico. I went out and hit shag balls, one after another. With every drive, I'd see the house I planned to buy for my mother.

When I got out of the army, I went back to Puerto Rico and showed the club members how I'd worked on my game—and how determined I was. Those men helped me get started on the PGA tournament circuit in 1960. It was slow-going at first, but in the 1963 Denver Open those forearm muscles of mine paid off. I won that tournament and Mama moved into her new home.

I played in a lot of tournaments after that, though I usually ended up making more friends than money. Before every tournament, we pros usually played practice rounds with club members. On one of these rounds, I met the famous psychiatrist Dr. Smiley Blanton, who was a member of the Sleepy Hollow Country Club in New York. A godly man who wrote many books on finding peace of mind through biblical principles, he helped found, with Norman Vincent Peale, what is known today as The Institutes of Religion and Health, which train clergy of all faiths for pastoral counseling and also treats people who need psychological and spiritual help.

Smiley Blanton was in his late seventies and I in my twenties, but when we'd walk the course, laughing and talking, those years between us didn't exist. He usually shot in the low eighties and could drive a ball two-hundred yards off the tee. I learned a lot from him. About life. About golf. He taught me that when I prepared to tee off, I must concentrate on the pin, not on the sand traps and water hazards in between.

"Be positive," he'd tell me. "Your body can do only what your brain sees, Chi Chi. If you think of the negatives, you'll be drawn to them. But if you keep your goal foremost in mind, you'll aim for it."

By the time I reached the age of fifty in 1985 and was eligible to join the Senior PGA Tour, I had won eight PGA tournaments in twenty-five years—a respectable record, though small change compared to the superstars. It didn't look as though I would take the senior circuit by storm either. I told friends that I was thinking about learning to hit shots off my knees. "I figure I have a better chance if I'm praying and swinging at the same time," I laughed ruefully.

I had a major problem with my putting. If anything kept me from winning big through the years, it was those last few feet before the cup. Putting is a decisive factor in winning championships. You have to drop those three- to six-footers consistently. And you must hole some of the long ones. Many a tournament is won by just one stroke.

By May of 1987 I was at a real low point. I had just blown another tournament. I mean I really blew it, missing about thirteen putts. I bogeyed and double bogeyed, shooting a forty-two on the last nine holes. I didn't even earn enough money in that tournament to cover expenses.

I felt lower than a drainage-ditch lizard in my old barrio in Rio Pedras. The next tournament was the Vantage at the Dominion Country Club in San Antonio, but I didn't have the heart for it. In fact, I was thinking of calling it quits. My wife and I flew to Dallas, and I said, "Iwalani, I'm going to put you on a plane for home, and I'm just going to sit here by myself in the airport hotel for three days and think." I wanted just to meditate; maybe God would show me something. And so I sat there in my room wondering if I should give up the game.

As I brooded, an hour passed, then two. I had never asked God for a win, only for the strength to accept whatever happened. But what *was* happening? I desperately searched for some kind of answer.

Suddenly it was as if God were talking inside of me. *Get out of here*, he said.

When God speaks, I listen. Just like when Papa would give an order, I learned to jump. With God I was even more attentive.

Get out of here.

I quickly packed my bags, and, walking in faith like Mama had taught, I took the next logical step and went to the airport. And since the next tournament seemed to be the place to head, I bought a ticket for San Antonio.

When I got to the gate to board the plane, who should be standing there but Bob Toski. My mouth fell open. Bob is one of America's top golf teachers. A champion pro player, he was on *Golf Digest* magazine's professional panel and has written books on the game.

He greeted me warmly.

After some small talk, I blurted. "Bob, would you help me with my putting?"

He looked at me for a moment, his friendly blue eyes crinkling. "Chi Chi," he smiled, "I was wondering how long it would take you to ask."

On the way to San Antonio, Bob gave me some pointers.

"First, you must look at your attitude toward putting," he said. "One simple problem is carelessness. This leads to really bad misses that then make you overly concerned. That generates more tension. And it becomes a vicious circle as you change your style and grasp at gimmicks; your stroke becomes mechanical and overcontrolled."

Then Bob mentioned something that reminded me of my old friend, Smiley Blanton. "Target projection," Bob called it. "Before you putt, always *see* the ball running up to and into the hole," he said. "Keep doing this and your subconscious will help you hole that putt."

I could just see Smiley's eyes twinkling behind his horn-rimmed glasses.

When we got onto the practice green, Bob watched me. After a bit, he suggested a small change in the way I handled my club.

"Your putter is traveling upward at impact instead of level or downward," he said. "That gives the ball a bad sidespin."

Bob encouraged me to hit slightly down on the ball and finish the stroke with my putter low to the ground. All it took was to position the ball a little farther back in my stance, making it easier to deliver a downward hit.

The result? I birdied six of nine practice holes, then went on to win that Vantage tournament. In the next three months I won five more big tournaments, earning in 1987 more than $500,000, plus the *Golf Digest* title of "Senior Player of the Year."

I gained a lot more than awards and titles from that experience. And I pass it on to the kids I teach in Clearwater, Florida, at my Chi Chi Rodriguez Youth Foundation for troubled, abused, and poor children. I tell them it's a lesson they can apply to any challenge they face. "First," I say, "communicate with God. *Listen* to him, and when you feel his direction, don't willy-wally around. *Obey.*"

The Lord sees a lot further down the course than we do. If I hadn't obeyed him that day in the hotel, I wouldn't have met Bob Toski at the airport.

Life is full of hazards and traps, I tell the kids. But if you keep your eye on the pin and follow through with all your might, you'll be a champion at everything you do, even if you don't win every time.

Yes, Chi Chi's my name, and through the grace of God, golf is still my game.

On the
Wings
of Faith

LIFE AFTER BASEBALL

DAVE DRAVECKY

Dave Dravecky, former San Francisco Giant, made a triumphant comeback from a public battle with cancer before having his arm amputated to stop the spread of the disease.

You may remember the video picture of me breaking my left arm as a result of a pitch I threw in Montreal on August 15, 1989. It seemed at the time as if the whole country saw the gruesome replay that kept showing on television. It was a big story. It was also the end of my baseball career.

Looking at the picture now, I can still feel the pain that seared through the whole left side of my body like a lightning bolt. I remember a collective gasp rising from the stands as I tumbled over in a writhing heap on the hard, blue-green Astro Turf, and the horrified looks of my teammates on the San Francisco Giants who raced to the mound—first baseman Will Clark, catcher Terry Kennedy, trainer Mark Letendre, manager Roger Craig. Even the Expos batter, Tim Raines, trotted out. He'd heard the sharp crack of my arm snapping, like a pistol shot, all the way at home plate, sixty feet, six inches away. And I remember closing my eyes and asking, "What can you possibly have in store for me now, Lord?"

It was a good question. That last pitch was more than the end of a playing career: it was the end of a sports drama that had played out over the previous weeks in front of a rapt national audience. It had culminated five days earlier, on August 10, in San Francisco's Candlestick Park, amid a deluge of media coverage, when I pitched—and won—my first major league game nearly a year after surgery for removal of a cancerous tumor in my pitching arm.

I will never forget the day Dr. George Muschler at the Cleveland Clinic diagnosed the tumor. It was September 23, 1988. My wife, Janice, was with me in the examining room as Dr. Muschler explained the surgery that would remove half of the deltoid muscle in my left arm, the large muscle that runs from your shoulder to your humerus bone.

Janice wanted to be very clear about what the doctors were telling us. "In other words," she said, her voice wavering slightly, "short of a miracle, Dave will never pitch again."

"That's right," Dr. Muschler replied sadly but absolutely. "Short of a miracle, he'll *never* pitch again."

God gave us that miracle. In the face of all odds, and without most of my deltoid muscle, I came back. The doctors couldn't figure out how I was doing it. They thought that after surgery I'd be lucky to be able to pull my wallet out of my back pocket. Just lifting my arm over my head would signal a remarkable recovery. Far from worrying about saving my career, they were focused on saving the *arm*. Yet in less than a year I was striking out major league hitters. Everyone called it unexplainable, but the explanation was clear to me. Dr. Muschler had said so himself: it could only be God answering prayer.

Why then, I wondered as I was carried off the field in Montreal that day, with players from both sides looking on in tears, had God done so much and brought me so far just to take back the miracle he'd given?

I'd been pitching baseball competitively since high school back in Boardman, Ohio, a quiet suburb of Youngstown. I did my hard time in the minor leagues, where pitching instructors gave me little chance of making the bigs. I endured dysentery and loneliness playing winter ball in South America. It was there, in Barranquilla, Colombia, during the darkest days of my career, that I began to develop a spiritual yearning for something more in my life than the baseball diamond. There had to be a greater plan.

A year later, struggling in lowly Double A ball in Amarillo, Texas, I met someone who helped me start to find an answer. He was my roommate, Byron Ballard, a likable young pitcher. The first thing I noticed about Byron was that he had hair the color of saffron, with freckles to match, and size fifteen feet. The other thing was that he spent most of his spare time reading and talking about the Bible. For a long time I listened and asked questions. Pretty soon I was reading the Bible too—devouring it. All that hot summer, while other players around me were cursing the hard, scorched infields and brutal game temperatures, the meager meal money and run-down motels, a change I had never dreamed of was transforming my life and putting the world into an entirely new and startling perspective.

So seven years later, when the bad news about my arm came from Dr. Muschler at the Cleveland Clinic, it had been the most natural thing in the world for Janice and me to pray for a healing. As painful as the thought was of giving up baseball in mid-career, a career I'd worked so hard to build and was just beginning to enjoy the fruits of, we understood it would be completely up to God if I made it back. When the doctors insisted it was impossible, Janice and I knew better and said so. We trusted in the Lord's plan, whatever it was.

When my arm broke after my big comeback game, I was disappointed—all that sweat and pain just to pitch a handful of innings. But angry, no. I knew that God must have something else in mind. What, I wasn't sure. But like any athlete, the prospect of retirement was tough. The career of a ballplayer is relatively short. For most of us, it is over far too soon. You grow up being a ballplayer; walking away from it in the prime of your life is the hardest thing you'll do, no matter how successful you've been. In the movie *Field of Dreams,* one of the phantom old-time ballplayers who vanishes mysteriously into the cornfield after each game cries out in a joking imitation of *The Wizard of Oz*'s Wicked Witch: "Help me! I'm melting!" Melting away—that's how the thought of leaving baseball sounds to those of us who have been fortunate enough to play the game.

On November 13, 1989, I announced my retirement, at the age of thirty-three. I'd broken my arm a second time that fall when I was inadvertently knocked to the field in the wild celebration that followed the Giants clinching the National League pennant. It was clear that without the deltoid muscle to help support it, my humerus bone was acutely vulnerable to stress fractures.

Not long after, doctors informed us that the tumor had returned. I would undergo another operation along with a new treatment that involved surgical implantation of "spikes" containing a small amount of radioactive material. This time I would lose the remainder of my deltoid muscle. In fact losing the whole arm was now a real and frightening possibility.

In the face of such an uncertain future, other things began happening in my life. I'd never particularly cared for all the media attention I got during my comeback. But the one good thing it did give me was a chance to say a few words publicly about my faith, and to set an example for other cancer patients, many of whom suffered far more serious forms of the disease than I. Now people were asking me to speak all over the country—at churches, hospitals, business meetings. I was a bit embarrassed at how much in demand I was. I wrote a book. Movie producers contacted me about doing my story. I was busier than ever.

It dawned on Janice and me that none of this could have happened if a small mysterious lump on my arm had not turned into something else. Which is not to say God gave me cancer—he didn't. But it was only through the love of God that I was led to find good in tragedy. The real miracle in my life was not that I came back from an impossible situation and played ball again. The real miracle in my life—in everyone's life—is that the Son of God came down to earth to suffer and die for our sins and redeem our souls. And that his love is always ready for us.

Inevitably there are times when I miss baseball, when I can practically hear the hum of the crowd as the players take the field. I see a game on television and immediately I am drawn into thinking how I would pitch the batter: slider on the outside corner of the plate, a change-up out of the strike zone, then *boom*, a fastball in on the hands. Keep 'em guessing. Sometimes it's just a feeling in the air on a humid summer night, the kind of night when a pitcher's arm can get warm and loose and great things might happen.

In the spring of 1991 Janice and I returned to Scottsdale, Arizona, where the Giants train. I was just along for the ride. Janice was speaking to a group of the baseball wives.

For a moment, when I first stepped into camp and heard the crack of wood on hard leather and saw a ball arc lazily into the deep desert sky, it was as if nothing had changed. I felt almost as if I could lace on my cleats again and go nine. But then just as quickly, before that ball smacked into the outstretched glove of a rookie outfielder, my separation from the game became crystallized and final, and I was at peace. It is a chapter of my life that's closed now. I am grateful for every second of it, especially those last few miraculous innings no one ever dreamed I'd get.

I've had several surgeries since my retirement. After each one there seems to be a little less of my left arm to save.

One thing I know. God never takes back a miracle. He just uses miracles in our lives to point the way.

My Search for *The Apostle*

Robert Duvall

Academy-Award winning actor Robert Duvall has performed in more than sixty-five films, including roles in The Godfather, Apocalypse Now, *and* The Apostle.

've been an actor all my working life, and learning a part has always meant more than just memorizing my lines. I immerse myself in the character I am to play. I find out everything I can about who he is, the world he comes from, his dreams, his fears, his passion, his humanity. I try to transform myself. A remarkable thing can happen in this process. Many times I discover something new about myself. Sometimes it is a discovery that changes my life.

In my recent movie, which I also wrote and directed, I play a troubled preacher who calls himself *The Apostle*. For years I have wanted to make this film. It's been a labor of love, and it began in 1962 when I prepared to play a character from the rural South in an off-Broadway play. To research the role I traveled to Hughes, Arkansas. Wandering the streets of the sleepy Delta town, hanging out in the coffee shop and the post office, I hoped to learn something about my character—from the way a man tipped his hat or drawled the directions to the local hotel. But what I never expected to find was something that would change how I looked at religion.

One Sunday as I strolled down the main drag I noticed people flocking to a simple white clapboard building, the local Pentecostal church. All sorts of folks, young and old, were going inside, where I could hear the clink of tambourines, the rap of a snare drum, and organ music rising. Might as well check this out, I thought. I slipped in and sat in back.

I grew up in a church-going Navy family. During World War II we lived in Annapolis, Maryland, while Dad commanded a destroyer escort in the North Atlantic, playing a deadly game of cat-and-mouse with German U-boats. Occasionally Mom woke up in the middle of the night with the overwhelming urge to pray for him. One morning at the breakfast table, she told us of the trouble she had sensed Dad was in. Later, we learned he had narrowly escaped being blown sky-high by a German torpedo during the night.

So I knew about the inner life of the Spirit, but I had never seen such an extraordinary outward expression of faith as I witnessed in that Pentecostal church. I had never seen church like that. People could barely contain the joy of their faith. Their faces were alive with it, imbued. Folks were on their feet, singing praise and clapping, shouting to God! The air crackled with the Spirit. It was nearly impossible to be a mere observer. I wanted to sing and shout with them. I couldn't explain it, but I knew the people in that church had a gift, a story to share. Somehow, someday, I would tell that story.

Soon after, my career boomed. I started working in movies, dozens of them, from *To Kill a Mockingbird* to *The Godfather*. I was fortunate to get some excellent roles. I wrote and directed a couple of films. Yet my interest in Pentecostalism never waned, incubating until I could figure out what to do with it. Then in 1981 I was cast as an evangelical preacher in a movie called *The Kingdom*. Again I immersed myself in my role. I made trips to small country churches all over the heartland, seeking out the incredible power of expressed faith I had felt in Hughes, soaking up all I could. But after months of preparation the film was canceled. I wondered what I would do with all I had learned.

In 1983 I won an Oscar for my portrayal of a down-and-out country singer who finds salvation in the film *Tender Mercies*. After I was named Best Actor I expected the offers to flood in. But my telephone was surprisingly quiet. There was a lull in my usually busy schedule.

I went home to Virginia, where my parents had retired and where I live when I'm not shooting a movie. My father had died and Mom was sick. My two brothers and I were trying to figure out what would be best for her, and I needed to be there. I kept thinking of my mother's faith and how it had sustained her during all the years Dad was at sea, how it had sustained all of us, how she prayed for me when I went off to New York to study acting. I was not a tortured artist from a troubled family; I had strong parents and a solid childhood. It seemed like only yesterday when we kids were fishing soft-shell crabs out of the bay, laughing and one-upping each other.

One day I sat at the desk in my father's wood-paneled den. Studying the walls, I was struck by his innate modesty. A rear admiral in the Navy, he had no plaques or medals displayed, none of his citations or awards for bravery. Everyone knew he was a hero. His career had spoken for itself. He believed in his country. I sat and wondered what I would be remembered for. Looking around my father's study and suddenly sensing the unyielding passage of time, I felt I needed to do something that had real meaning for me, before it was too late. Something I believed in. I took out a legal pad and began writing a story, the one I had wanted to write for many years.

It was a story of a preacher. A good man but a flawed one—flawed as we all are. Called by God at the age of twelve, he becomes a respected minister with a rousing gift for charismatic preaching. But his family is torn apart by marital infidelity. In a dreadful moment of jealous rage he injures a man and runs. His flight becomes a journey toward a redeemed faith, a return to God's saving grace. Assuming a new identity, he starts a church deep in the Louisiana bayou. Again his gift for preaching sweeps up a congregation, returning faith to a town where it had lagged, but his own redemption can come only when he faces the truth of his transgressions.

What was most important to me was to make a movie where Christianity was treated on its own terms, with the respect it deserves. Hollywood usually shows preachers as hucksters and hypocrites, and I was sick and tired of that. I wanted to show the joy and vitality I had seen with my own eyes and felt in my heart and in my life, the sheer, extraordinary excitement of faith. I especially wanted to capture the rich flavor, the infectious cadences and rhythm of good, down-home, no-holds-barred preaching.

The story seemed to flow from me. I wrote everywhere, in airports and hotels, on the set between scenes, even in meetings. But writing a screenplay is one thing. Getting it produced is something else altogether. I took my script to Hollywood producers, and was met with the same response: "Bob, religion is not a subject our audiences want to watch." I disagreed. Why wouldn't audiences want to watch a movie about something that is foremost in so many people's lives?

I kept gathering material for the film and reworking the script. Near my house in Virginia I met an astounding ninety-three-year-old preacher named Isham Williams. "If I was any younger I'd make that movie with you," he declared. I was even more impressed when preachers I met said I could use anything I wanted from their sermons. No squabbles about copyright or screen credit. James Robison, one of the greatest, gave me free run [of his sermons]. I adapted one of his most powerful sermons for the penultimate scene.

I called the film *The Apostle*—what my protagonist, Sonny, calls himself when he sets up his new church. In my research I was drawn several times to Memphis. Once, I attended a conference of believers, where I overheard the phrase I used when Sonny prays: "I always call You Jesus, and You always call me Sonny."

I wasn't getting anywhere with Hollywood, yet my work on the movie filled my soul. One Sunday in New York I visited six churches, ending up at Harlem's vast Abyssinian Baptist Church. There in a packed congregation before a huge choir, when we all began to sing "What a Friend We Have in Jesus," I found myself connected to the Lord in a way I had never felt before, deep within me. Yes, I thought, we're all kin through Jesus. Not just what we read about him in the Bible, but who he is. That was the secret to powerful faith, the power I wanted to convey in my movie.

I told anybody who would listen, "Even if I can't get some big money from a studio, I've got to make this movie." The next thing I knew my accountant called me up and said, "I know this is an important project for you, Bob. I've been poring over your finances and you've finally gotten to the point where you can afford to spend a chunk of your money." He is a very conservative accountant, so I knew I was getting the green light!

In the end, that's what I did. Some of my Pentecostal friends tell me my urgings were the Holy Spirit's doing. I'm inclined to agree with them. In an amazingly swift seven-week period we filmed *The Apostle*, all on location in Louisiana. The things I worried about never came to pass. Generators didn't break down, the weather was good, people showed up on time, no one got sick.

I'm proud of the film. Many of the parts are played by real people and real preachers, not professional actors, because true faith is something that's hard to duplicate. I think some viewers might be shocked—pleasantly so, I hope—to hear Jesus' name mentioned so often, or startled by the unironic tone of the church scenes and worship services. They might be surprised to see blacks and whites worshiping together as equals even in the deepest rural South. Mostly, I hope they will be moved—moved the way I was when I happened upon that small church in Hughes, Arkansas, and, with no warning, something awakened within me that had always been there, dormant and untouched until that day. It was the greatest discovery I ever made.

I'm a Free Man Now

JOHNNY CASH

Johnny Cash recorded his first single with Sun Records in 1955;
his music career spans more than five decades and 1,500 recordings.

Now I looked at the old man. He looked like he was behind bars. But I knew that I was the one behind the bars, only I didn't know where the jail was or how I got there.

The old man said, "Let me know when you're ready."

I forced myself to sit up. "I'm ready now."

Ready for what? I wasn't sure why I'd been arrested. I figured it had something to do with the pills. Once before, the pills had put me behind bars, but that time I was lucky.

That was in 1965. I had gone into Mexico to get a supply of the pills I felt I needed to stay alive. As I was re-entering at El Paso, the customs inspector found the pills. That time I spent a day in jail. Because it was my first arrest, the judge let me off with a year's suspended sentence. There was a newspaper reporter in the courtroom; his story went out on the wires, and that's how people found out I was an addict.

A lot of people already knew. By then, I had been on pills five years. I took pep pills to turn me on enough to do a show. Then I took depressants to calm down enough to get some sleep. That, at least, was what my friends said. They said I was working too hard and traveling too much and trying to squeeze too much out of every day. They said maybe I should take some time off.

I thought I knew better. I tried pep pills the first time because they happened to be available one day when I was in the mood for a new kick. The high they gave me was beautiful. I felt I owned the world, and the world was perfect during those lofty moments. I couldn't believe that a couple of little pills could contain so much beauty and joy. I stayed on pills because they made me feel great. If people wanted to give excuses for my habit, I let them.

Then I began to realize that the highs were getting lower. The few pills I was on every day weren't enough anymore. I had to go from a few to several, then to dozens. Still that old feeling wasn't there. I was always nervous and tense and irritable. I didn't want to eat. I couldn't sleep. I started losing weight.

So I went on depressants, looking for lows, looking for peace. When I found peace, I couldn't trust it because I knew it was a fleeting peace. Soon I would crave getting high, and the highs would not come to me.

After the El Paso mess, I took an apartment with a friend who was also on pills. One day when my supply ran out, I remembered that he had some in his car. He was asleep and I couldn't find his keys, so I went out and broke into the car. When he later accused me of this, I denied it violently and we almost fought. He knew I was lying, and I knew he did. The next day, I admitted it, and he said he understood. We were like two cowardly kids forgiving each other for being afraid of the dark.

In time, I became afraid of everything. I would be a nervous wreck before a show; I was never sure of myself during a performance; I didn't believe people when they said things had gone all right. Sometimes I was too sick to work. Sometimes I didn't even show up. It didn't take booking agents long to stop risking their money on me. Even though I knew this meant a loss of income to others in the show, people who were good friends, I didn't care. I didn't care about anything.

I knew I was killing myself. I had seen drugs kill others. Whatever drug an addict is hooked on, he has to keep increasing his daily dosage to feel anywhere near normal. This is the nature of addiction. The day comes when he takes the overdose that kills him. Knowing this, I accepted early death as the inescapable fate of addicts: there was just no other way out. Even when I thought of all the things I had to be thankful for, I could find no hope for myself, no chance for change.

I was twelve, I remembered, when electricity came to the small Arkansas farm where I was raised. Dad bought a radio, and I'll never forget the first Saturday night I heard the exciting country music from the Grand Ole Opry, in Nashville. That moment, I discovered my future. Right away, I started writing my own country songs, and I told everybody I was going to become an entertainer. I guess only my mother believed me. We were poor, and so she took in laundry to pay for a few voice lessons. At seventeen, I earned my first money at performing: the fifteen-dollar first prize in an amateur contest. Then I learned to play the guitar.

In 1954, I attended a radio-announcing school, hoping that becoming a disc jockey might open doors to performing. To earn a living, I sold housewares door-to-door. I got to know guitarist Luther Perkins and bassist Marshall Grant. We put together an act; we rehearsed a lot; we worked whenever we could, whether or not we got paid. After a year, we agreed that the only way we could find out if we were ready for the Big Time was to audition for somebody big.

We auditioned for Sun Records, which led to our first recording. This led to a two-year contract at the Grand Ole Opry. We made more recordings. We went on the road. We became known. By 1960 we had advanced enough to put together a show of our own. Then I moved on to the high of pills.

By 1967, I was on the verge of a nervous breakdown, and I knew it. I was usually on a hundred pills a day, but I got no pleasure from them, no peace. I couldn't stand my life, but I couldn't find my way out of it. One day my friends talked to me about entering a mental institution, and the thought of that completely shattered me. I got into my car, well supplied with pills, and headed south. I remember crossing the Georgia border. Next thing I knew, I was staring at a ceiling and an elderly jailer was asking me if I felt better.

I got up. He unlocked the door. I asked, "How did I get here?"

He said, "One of the night men found you stumbling around the streets. He brought you in so you wouldn't hurt yourself."

I followed him down a corridor and into his office, and I asked, "How much time do you think I'll get for this?"

He shook his head. "You're doing time right now, Johnny, the worst kind." He handed me an envelope. "Here are your things." As I was putting things into my pockets, he said, "I'm a fan of yours, Johnny. I've always admired you. It's a shame to see you ruining yourself. I didn't know you were this bad off."

I'd heard that sad song before, from concerned friends. I said, "Yeah. Sure."

He said, "I don't know where you think you got your talent from, Johnny, but if you think it came from God, then you're sure wrecking the body he put it in."

I said, "Yeah. Sure. Thanks. Can I go now?" He nodded.

That morning, as I stepped into the warm sunshine, I took a quick but deep look at my life over the past seven years, and I knew that I was a better man than that.

Maybe it was the reference to God that suddenly cleared my mind. I had been raised by religious parents; faith had always meant a lot to me; I have tried to express it in some of my songs. But until that morning it hadn't occurred to me to turn to God for help in kicking my habit.

I remembered this verse: "Know ye not that your body is the temple of the Holy Ghost which is in you, which ye have of God, and ye are not your own?" (1 Corinthians 6:19, KJV). This helped convince me that I must try to break my habit. But how?

And I remembered this: God had given me a free will, and I had freely used it in deciding to experiment with the drugs, which had now robbed me of it. I realized that to be free again I would need all the willpower I could acquire, and I knew this power could come only from God, who had created me free. I asked him to go to work on me, then and there.

Back in Nashville, I went to June Carter and Marshall Grant, and I told them, "I'm kicking pills, as of now. I don't expect it to be easy, so I'll need your help. See to it that I eat regular meals. See to it that I keep regular hours. If I can't sleep, sit and talk to me. If we run out of talk, then let's pray."

We prayed a lot. I am a free man now, as I have been since that morning when I discovered that I could be once again.

Because of the kind of work I do, it is difficult to sweep past mistakes under the rug. Every once in a while, I meet some youngster who knows I used to be an addict, as he is now, and he asks me what he can do to kick his habit. I tell him what I learned, "Give God's temple back to him. The alternative is death."

A FAIRY TALE COME TRUE

JAHJA LING

Jahja Ling left his home in Indonesia at the age of eighteen to study at Juilliard. He has since conducted nearly every major orchestra in North America, Europe, and Asia.

It's a long, long way from Indonesia to Ohio and from leading a church choir in Jakarta to conducting the Cleveland Orchestra at Severance Hall. Sometimes when I think back over my long journey, I am still amazed at the way it happened. I remember my father, and Miss Lee, and Professor Munz; and I remember the sometimes mysterious coincidences that made it possible.

I grew up in Jakarta. My father, who at the time was independently wealthy, worked in civil service, first under the Dutch colonial government and then for the Republic of Indonesia. He loved everything Dutch and European—particularly music. My two sisters and I grew up listening to Bach, Beethoven, and Chopin, and to my father talking about the great pianist and conductor, Arthur Rubinstein. So because of him I developed a love of music early on.

Then there was Miss Tse-Siu Lee. In those prosperous days, our mansion was so large that my parents invited Miss Lee to conduct her kindergarten class in some of the rooms. We all loved Miss Lee. I can still picture her: a tall middle-aged woman, with graying hair fixed in a bun, wearing a long, traditional Chinese dress. She was so gentle, so caring, so loving.

Miss Lee was also a devout Christian. Although my father practiced ancestor worship at a shrine in our house, he allowed Miss Lee to teach us hymns and read us wonderful Bible stories and tell us about the God-man Jesus, who had lived long ago and had died for our sins.

My parents even allowed Miss Lee to enroll us in a Chinese-Christian Sunday school. Because of her, my sisters and I eventually accepted Christ publicly; then my mother came to believe. Finally my father himself became a Christian.

By coincidence, Miss Lee came to have another important influence on me. My grandmother had purchased an expensive German Ibach piano for my older sister. After she lost interest in her lessons, it stood collecting dust for several years—until Miss Lee began playing it for our kindergarten class. I was only four, but I was fascinated by the big piano and watched Miss Lee. How did she create such beautiful sounds?

One day during class, I climbed onto the stool and played "Choo-Choo Train" by ear. I was only imitating what I had seen Miss Lee do, but Miss Lee saw something else. She went to my parents and said, "This child has a special gift from the Lord. He must have teachers."

By the time I was five, I was playing for the Sunday school and for Christmas pageants and other events. I had a tall stool in order to reach the keys. Visitors would come to watch. My parents were silent but proud. So was Miss Lee.

About this time there was an economic collapse in Indonesia. My father lost nearly everything. We had to leave our lovely big house and servants and the easy life.

A few years later, in 1959, when I was eight, Miss Lee went back to China. We were all in tears the day we saw her off. "Be a good boy, Jahja," she said in her soft voice, leaning down and brushing my hair back. "God has given you a wonderful talent. You must develop it! Study, work hard, have faith. I will remember you in my prayers."

Over the next eight years I did work hard, and I won competitions. By the time

I was in my teens I was also conducting our church choir. And though piano was then paramount in my life, one day I casually asked my teacher, Rudy Laban, about studying orchestra conducting. "Forget it, Jahja!" he replied. "It's the most difficult thing to study. Impossible!"

Even before I graduated from high school, my teachers and people at church were telling me I must study abroad. One of my friends was going to Vienna to study architecture. His father urged me to go along. I rushed home and told my parents.

My father listened patiently and then said sadly, "Jahja, we just can't afford it. I'm sorry." That ended the discussion. In my culture, children don't argue with parents—ever. Or share deep longings.

I remember leafing through music-school catalogs and dreaming, especially about Juilliard, in New York. But you had to fly to America just to audition, and that was impossible.

I continued to work and study—and pray. I applied to other schools, and for scholarships. "Have faith," Miss Lee had said. I was trying. I waited. Eventually I was accepted by the Manhattan School of Music, and I received a Rockefeller grant to pay my way.

While all this was going forward, I won the Jakarta Piano Competition. As part of the prize, I would perform with the Jakarta Symphony—my "farewell concert" in Indonesia.

On the first day of rehearsal, by chance a stranger was sitting in the concert hall. He was Mieczyslaw Munz, a famous professor from Juilliard. Munz was vacationing in Jakarta.

As I rehearsed a Grieg piano concerto, he sat there without comment. But afterward he was heard to say, "Very good. I want to have him go to Juilliard."

Juilliard? It was a fairy tale come true.

In America I plunged happily into my studies and adapted myself to my new country. On Sundays I attended a Chinese-American church in Manhattan, where I began leading the choir.

About two years later I received a sad letter from my parents: Miss Lee had been killed in Communist China by the notorious Red Guards during the Cultural Revolution.

I was stunned. I cried for a long time.

In the course of my studies at Juilliard, I began to think about conducting again and took an elective in it under John Nelson. But the school kept turning me down for a major in conducting.

"Jahja, why don't you look into Yale?" suggested one of my school friends.

Yale? The very name was intimidating, but I applied, along with sixty or more others. Twelve of us auditioned for the great teacher Otto Werner Mueller, who would select only one new pupil.

The first day of the audition seemed to prove out Laban's warnings back in Jakarta—that conducting for me was impossible. Professor Mueller paced before us—all six-foot-seven of him, with bushy Beethoven hair flying out in all directions. He was a frightening figure.

"You arrogant people!" he thundered. "Who do you think you are? Do you have the effrontery to think Almighty God has appointed *you* to lead others?"

Then for two gruelling hours he tested our ear training and musical knowledge.

"In the beginning of Brahms's "Haydn variations," what is the contrabass doing? Up-bow or down-bow?"

I knew immediately it was a trick question. The bow is neither up nor down. The contrabassist plucks the strings. Oh, he had all sorts of tricky questions.

When we accompanied him, he said my playing was "heavy." In my private interview he growled, "You're in America. Do you know how to play 'The Star-Spangled Banner'? Harmonize it!"

Oh, that's easy, I thought. It's in B-flat.

"Transpose it into F-sharp major!"

And, when I finished: "Tomorrow you will conduct the orchestra in Brahms's 'Haydn variations.'" Then, almost as an afterthought: "And also a symphony, uh . . . Beethoven's Second, first movement. Prepare for these overnight."

Overnight? He couldn't be serious!

After hours of intense study that night, I could no longer focus on the notes. It was too much. Sure, I had talent. But so did others. Who *did* I think I was?

If only Miss Lee were here! I thought. She would know what to do!

Miss Lee would pray, a voice in my mind gently whispered. Of course! Her last words to me were, "Jahja, have faith. I will remember you in my prayers."

Folding my hands on the open music and bowing my head I whispered, "Dear Lord, I don't *think* I'm arrogant. I don't want to be. Calm my fears. Be with me tomorrow. I can't do it without You."

Sitting there in that dormitory room, I suddenly had a new perspective on things. I didn't just "happen" to have a father who loved music, and we just didn't "happen" to have a piano. Miss Lee didn't "happen" to come to live and teach at our home or lead me to Christ or discover my talent. And Professor Munz didn't just "happen" to be in Jakarta when he heard me play. No, all those "coincidences" were part of a plan. They were the Lord's doing. If this was God's timing, I had to be ready. With new confidence I turned back to the music scores on the desk before me.

The next afternoon I was nervous. But once I raised my baton I lost track of time. How can I describe it? The music in both selections, in turns soft then powerful, lovely then wrenching, poured out from the orchestra and seemed to wash over me in waves—waves that I was mentally and physically *drawing* from the musicians. It wasn't arrogance. It was something mystical, almost holy.

When I brought my baton down at the final crashing notes of the Beethoven movement, I paused a moment, spent by the effort. There was a smattering of applause from the few spectators in the hall. I turned to Professor Mueller. His stern look had been replaced by something like respect, maybe amazement.

As I look back on it now, I know my audition at Yale *was* God's timing. I became Professor Mueller's student, and I embarked on a career as a musical conductor that eventually brought me to Cleveland to one of the world's best orchestras.

"Study, work hard, have faith," Miss Lee had said.

And, she might have added, if you do, God will provide the opportunities and the means to fulfill your dreams.

WHAT FATHER KNOWS NOW

ROBERT YOUNG

Film and television actor Robert Young is best known for his roles in the hit TV series,
Father Knows Best *and* Marcus Welby, M.D.

hen our first daughter was born, my wife, Betty, and I prided ourselves on being enlightened parents. We hoped for a large family and had decided to be very modern, very intellectual with our children. They were to have something we called "Christian standards" by which, I suppose, we meant ethics. And to direct the children in the right direction, we decided each would be christened in a nonsectarian church; but no church ties would be forced upon them: they were to be allowed to choose for themselves.

I realize now that it would have been difficult to offer them any other course, since we had never made the choice ourselves. I had been accepted into the Baptist church at the age of ten; but the only impressions my memory retained were the rite of immersion, the ability to recite the Books of the Old Testament, and a good attendance record at Sunday school for about two years. A flood in Kentucky had destroyed the church record in the town where my wife was born and her mother could never rightly remember whether Betty was baptized a Congregationalist or a Methodist.

As a young married couple we didn't worry about this, for we attended church only at the fashionable times of the year: Christmas and Easter. When I thought about it at all, I felt no need for constant church affiliation.

But we did want our children to have those Christian standards!

Thus, each of our four daughters in order of their appearance—Carol Ann, Barbara, Betty Lou, and Kathy—were christened in a lovely ceremony right in our living room by the minister of the Beverly Hills Community Church. And right there my ignorance was showing; had I entered the church proper, as I have since done, I would have observed on the bulletin board that the denomination was Presbyterian. But I didn't. Betty and I simply assumed that a community church was nonsectarian.

Once the girls were christened, we followed point two of our plan. Their mother and I tried to surround them with a closely knit, loving family atmosphere; we heard their prayers regularly, for we were praying people ourselves.

"You are," I told my daughters proudly, "free to choose your own religion." But I was as foolish as I was wrong. No real choice was being offered them, no habit of churchgoing was being developed.

Fourteen years—fourteen long years—elapsed before any one of the children decided upon anything or even mentioned a specific church. Then from boarding school Carol Ann wrote us a letter. Would we mind, she inquired, if she joined the Episcopal Church?

"It isn't sudden," wrote Carol Ann. "I've always had a tremendous respect for our chaplain, and I must admit it was his faith that made him what he is. So I began studying the service, trying to understand the words and the symbolism, and now they have great meaning for me. I truly love the service, and it gives me something I need."

A few weeks later we attended her confirmation.

During that summer vacation, each Sunday while mother and father and all her younger sisters slept, our fifteen-year-old daughter rose quietly and went to All Saints Church in Beverly Hills. Then, out of deference to Carol Ann, Betty and I began attending with her. The younger girls, still free to make their choice, now chose to get up and go to church school.

In one short summer we became a churchgoing family!

At first I, personally, felt strange; I had not been to church in a long time. Carol Ann's return to school left us on our own, yet still we went. Why? Because it began to seem important, that's why.

Then one Sunday morning an adult confirmation class was announced. Here again my ignorance was evident. Somehow, I had thought that after one reached a certain age one was too old to be confirmed . . . nor was I sure I wanted permanent membership.

I listened to the reassuring statement that the curious and the weary, were welcome, temporarily or permanently.

As Betty and I attended the class, we began to learn things, to feel a part of the group; and when the instruction period ended, we went right on into full church membership.

We had made our decision.

Our three remaining daughters were still offered their freedom of choice, but with this difference—our own choice had given them a real choice, churchgoing had become a reality. It was a thing you did, not something you just talked or wondered about.

How can you teach a child the necessity to make a choice if you haven't found it necessary to make one yourself? Talk does not place values anywhere. If we wanted our children to place God in the center of their lives, to have lasting Christian standards, then worship was not a question of forcing something on them but of offering them an opportunity, and of availing ourselves of the same privilege.

Has being a churchgoing family made a difference in our lives?

We feel it has.

There has been no dramatic sinner-to-saint conversion. Fortunately we did not insist on miracles. But we have grown into a greater unity with one another and our fellow man, and there is a new steadiness and stability in our family life. It has been easier to discuss our problems in terms of our relationship to God.

The first thing it did for me personally was to rid me of a vast store of ignorance—the sly rumors I'd accepted almost unconsciously that "church people" are stuffy, no fun at a party and that Sunday school teachers and clergymen are pompous and dull. I found our church filled with people much like ourselves, a mixture of problems, good will, humor, and shortcomings, but banded together to help one another and to be helped to do something about our difficulties. I gained insight into my own shortcomings, and I began to overcome self-consciousness when I thought or spoke in terms of God, Jesus Christ, God's will, God's children.

To me, church membership has meant instruction and activity, theory put into practice. I found I had a lot to learn, some of it uncomfortable, but all of it invaluable.

I think what amazed me most was that I could live all those years with a real need for church and not know it. I have been a church member for five short years now and I am still asking, "Why did I wait so long?" I guess perhaps the answer is that father *didn't* know best.

Many legitimate opportunities for activity and service have come to me through church membership, and very often I've felt shy, or too new. As, for instance, when our minister tapped me to serve on the vestry.

"I don't know how," I said. "I'm a beginner at all this."

"You're on the Board of Directors of Bishop's School, aren't you?" he demanded.

"But that's different," I protested.

"Not much," he replied firmly. "Here's your do-it-yourself kit," and he handed me a neat volume called "How to Become a Vestryman."

Recently, I was asked to serve as consultant to the Radio and Television Division of the Episcopal Church, and Betty has been very active with the church-sponsored Neighborhood Youth Association. Now, none of this has been the dramatic, soul-saving activity I anticipated when I first joined the church, yet from every task which we have undertaken, Betty and I have gotten solid satisfaction and felt very humble to have been offered an opportunity to serve.

In taking stock, we became even more fully aware that our lives have been full of blessings and answered prayer. I think my reaction has been much like that of our youngest daughter, Kathy, who knelt to say her evening prayers with us shortly after her ninth birthday. She asked blessings for everyone—her mother, myself, her sisters, the neighbors, her school teacher, and the dogs. Then she started on her request list. That was pretty long too. It sounded like an enthusiastic letter to Santa Claus. Suddenly there was a pause and then I heard Kathy say, in a small, meek voice: "And now, dear God, is there anything I can do for you?"

THE GREEN GROCER

JOE CARCIONE

A produce man by trade, Joe Carcione became known as the "Green Grocer" following his nationally televised spots highlighting what produce was fresh and in-season.

The American dream. Its bright hope drew my parents to this country from Sicily. Its challenge inspired me to reach for the stars in building my own produce company. And then one day my dream got squashed.

Since January 1933, when I began working in San Francisco's produce terminal, sweeping floors and lugging crates among other duties, the fresh fruit and vegetable wholesale business has been my life. I'd learned it from my father, who could almost tell what an orange was thinking. He knew when produce was at its best and when to avoid it. "Pepino," he'd tell me, "buy the ripe strawberries, not the ones with the green shoulders. The red ones have all the sweetness that the good Lord said they should have."

Every night I'd fall into bed almost too tired to say my prayers. But I loved the work and the dark, misty dawn when farm trucks groaned up to the sidewalks of the old San Francisco market under dew-glistening loads of iceberg lettuce, Santa Rosa plums, and Valencia oranges.

I learned to pick out the best-quality produce. I loved the cheerful haggling with produce buyers and the deals you closed with a handshake; and I loved the afternoons when I'd be phoning growers: "You're *sure* our load of asparagus is coming in tomorrow?"

Finally, in 1958, I was able to start my own company, Best Fruit and Produce.

For many years I would get up every morning between one and two to be at the market on time. It was providing a good living for my wife, Madeline, our three children, and me.

In order to increase the sales of my produce, I bought advertising on the radio station KCBS in San Francisco. In time, the program director of the station asked me to make a report every Monday through Friday about what was fresh and good in the market that day. I was surprised. I told him I had never been on radio before. He suggested that I try it. I did. And I have been on that radio station every day since 1967.

I am not a sophisticated man; my voice is pure North Beach Italian-American and somewhat raspy. But then, God made me like I am. So I figured I would just be myself. I found myself talking by telephone directly from the terminal on an informational spot called "The Man on the Produce Market."

I spoke to listeners just like I'd talk to a friend. I told them how to spot spoiled or unripe fruit, how to test vegetables for freshness and quality, how to find good buys and gave tips on serving them.

People liked it and soon San Francisco's *Chronicle* asked me to write a daily column, which became known as "The Green Grocer." It helped people become more aware of the value of fresh fruits and vegetables. Then one morning I was checking a load of Tokay grapes. They were flame red and sweet. I was sampling one when someone shouted: "Hey Joe, telephone."

My bank was calling. "Could you come in this afternoon, Mr. Carcione?"

In the bank's quiet office I received surprising news. After closing the door behind them, two bank officials sat down with me. "Joe, it's not just that your account is overdrawn, but . . ."

"Overdrawn?" I stared at them. "By how much?"

"Somewhere around a hundred thousand dollars."

I shot forward in my chair. I couldn't believe it. There had to be a mistake. My accountant—he handled all my company's complex finances. The payroll records, bank deposits, taxes. He would know. Then I remembered. He had not been in the office for the past two days. Someone said he had called in sick. I called him. There was no answer.

When I finally got home, I could hardly talk to Madeline about it. But even then I had no idea of how bad things were.

Within a week I knew. Our Social Security and federal withholding taxes had not been paid. On top of that, over one hundred-fifty-thousand dollars had been siphoned off. We were short a half-million dollars!

The accountant? This man I had known and trusted had simply disappeared.

For six months I struggled to keep Best Fruit and Produce going, but it had been dealt a fatal blow. "Joe," my lawyer said sadly, "I know it's tough, but there's only one thing you can do."

"Not bankruptcy?"

He nodded.

Late that night when I stumbled into the house, I told Madeline all about it. "Babe," I quavered, my voice breaking, "I don't understand how it all happened, but . . . but we may lose our house."

Madeline gave me a long hug and said softly: "Don't worry, Joe; we've lived in worse places."

Without her encouragement I don't know what I would have done. Even so, I was not prepared for the trauma of the bankruptcy proceedings, the court appearances, and the deep shame. It nearly killed me to see everything I'd struggled for sold under the auctioneer's hammer: all our trucks, dock equipment, and office furniture.

On the last day I walked alone through the packing shed. It was still redolent with the tangy scent of oranges and the fragrance of bell peppers and green beans. It was also full of memories.

Now everything was gone. Even the radio program and newspaper column seemed meaningless.

I went home and walked past Madeline directly into our bedroom, where I fell onto the bed. Thirty-four years down the drain. I thought of my family and my parents who were so proud of me. Now what would they think of the one who had to declare bankruptcy?

As I lay there thinking of my family, I remembered my grandmother. I could again see her in her black satin dress, slowly working her way up the street to attend mass at Saint Peter and Paul. After her sight gave out, neighbors gently guided her. But every morning she went, no matter the weather.

I couldn't understand her tenacity and asked my mother, "Isn't it about time she took a rest from all that?"

My mother's brown eyes became thoughtful and she said: "She is an old woman, yes. Her husband is gone and she lives with memories. But she goes to give God what she has: her prayers, her faith, and her gratefulness."

She gently squeezed my shoulder. "Every day she thanks him for making the dream come true."

I lay there in the bedroom thinking of that dream—the American dream they called it—that brought them to this country.

I remembered my father looking at me levelly. "You know, Joe, back in the old country some people thought gold could be picked up in the streets here." He chuckled. "They soon found out that things were different. But the dream, the real American dream, was that over here you . . ." He looked out toward the Bay. "Well, I'll tell you; back there whatever your father did, you followed in his footsteps, whether he was a fisherman or ran a fruit stand. Over here, if you work hard enough, you have the freedom and the opportunity to make of yourself anything you want."

Lying on the bed I thought of the man who came to this country with nothing, nothing but hope, determination, and a deep trust in God.

Suddenly, I felt ashamed for lying on my back like a defeated man when I already had so much: a wonderful wife, fine children, and a knowledge of fruits and vegetables that nobody could take away from me. And all the while here I was acting as though money were the American dream. "Well, it's not," I said, almost out loud, "it's not."

I jumped up, ran into the kitchen where Madeline was stirring spaghetti sauce, and grabbed her around the waist. "Hey, babe," I shouted, "to heck with bankruptcy, to heck with the past. There's nothing anyone can do about it. We're going to fight back and we're going to come out all right!"

Her blue eyes shone and she kissed me, spilling spaghetti sauce down my shirt. I felt like a boy again.

Maybe I had lost the produce business, but I still had the radio program and newspaper column. And through them, I could help others.

When I did my next radio program from the market and wrote my newspaper column, I completely forgot the past.

"Folks," I waxed enthusiastic, "you gotta believe me, we have pineapples in here this morning that are out of this world. They'll be in your supermarket later today. You know, folks, a golden ripe pineapple has a marvelous fragrance. If you put it in the trunk of your car, in a very short while it will fill your car with its wonderful aroma. That's one way the pineapple tells you it's ripe and ready for eating. Most of the time a green pineapple has no aroma at all."

When something needed criticizing, I called a spade a spade. "The price of iceberg lettuce is out of sight today, folks," I'd warn. "Don't buy it; buy cabbage. It's cheap and plentiful, and it has more vitamins and minerals."

"More and more people are tuning in, Joe," said the program director, "and research shows that listeners love you."

Not everybody loved me. Marketing produce is a rough and tumble business, and I had my share of critics among growers, wholesalers, and retailers.

Then I overheard a wholesaler: "So he puts the knock on a bad shipment of tomatoes. But he can turn around and rave about grapes and the buyer impact is felt almost immediately. So we hate him one day and love him the next."

Two years after my radio debut, I was asked to make a television appearance. From that developed a regular weekly show on San Francisco's Channel 4, KRON-TV. Again I was scared. I'm not the most handsome guy in the world.

It worked. Within a few years the television spot was syndicated. By 1984 my *Green Grocer* show was seen regularly by more than seven million people in sixty-five different cities across the nation.

At age sixty-nine I'm having more fun and excitement than ever. I run a small fruit exporting business. With the growing demand for fresh, natural goods, I'm having the time of my life helping folks pick the finest fruits and vegetables for the money and giving out my favorite old-country recipes. I even found time to write two books, *The Consumers Guide to Fruits & Vegetables* and *The Green Grocer*.

That accountant? I don't know what happened to him. *Vengeance is mine; I will repay, saith the Lord* (Romans 12:19, KJV). And I have long left him to God. In fact, when I think of all the fun I'm having today, I wonder. Maybe the guy even did me a favor?

So let me tell you something. The American dream is as true today as when it attracted our forefathers. It is the freedom to grow as much as we're able. It is the opportunity to rise up when we are flat on our backs and begin again. And it works best when we concentrate on our God-given talents. Mine is to tell people about radishes and cauliflowers. Yours may be being a housewife, typing letters, or helping build houses.

But when we concentrate on the giving and the trusting, it puts us in the best position to reap his blessings. So remember, *buon appetito. Salute per cento anni!* (Good health for one hundred years.)

READY FOR PRIME TIME

CATHERINE HICKS

Catherine Hicks made her television debut in 1976. Since that time she has acted on stage, in films, and in television series, including 7th Heaven.

Seven years ago I was at a crossroads. My acting career had stalled, and I faced some tough financial decisions. I was forty-three years old, and it looked like everything I'd worked so hard to build was falling apart. Perhaps you're thinking I asked God for help. But I couldn't even put into words what I needed from God. No, just like at two earlier critical points in my life, it was instead he who spoke to me.

The first of these crises came while I was in college at Notre Dame University in South Bend, Indiana. A big part of what drew me to Notre Dame was the chance to be a cheerleader for a legendary football team. In high school I had fallen in love with cheerleading—the electric thrill of being up in front of a crowd and the sense of belonging I felt at the games.

At Notre Dame, every day after class I spent hours practicing dance and gymnastics. I went to all the games and got to know a lot of the players and cheerleaders. "Please, God," I'd pray at Mass, "let me make the squad." I gave my all at tryouts that spring and waited for the list of names of those who'd made the cut to be posted.

On the morning the names went up, I jumped out of bed, ran up to the gymnasium door, and scanned the list for my name. I didn't see it. I looked again. I didn't make it.

It turned out that I had missed getting on the team by only one vote. I was crushed all the same. All my ideas about who I was, where I fit in, and how my life would be had been shattered. Now what? I tried to throw myself into my classwork, but I couldn't shake myself out of my disappointment. My grades dipped, and I pulled back from my friends.

"You've got to come to the frat party with me tonight, Cathy," a dorm-mate insisted one night.

I finally gave in and went, but it was almost like I was watching myself from afar, talking and laughing but feeling nothing. Soon I made an excuse and walked out into the chilly night. Shivering as a brisk wind slapped the trees, I ducked into the chapel to warm up. It was empty, and the lights were dim and comforting. I breathed in the musky smell of candlewax and flowers.

All those times I'd prayed for God to help me make the cheerleading team . . . now I didn't know what to ask for anymore. There was just a deep inexpressible need for something. Into that need, as raw as an open wound, came a soothing calm. *Trust me*, God seemed to say; and all at once I felt that, as hopeless as things seemed at the time, life would somehow be good again.

As I headed back to my dorm, I noticed a long line of people going into the campus theater. The marquee read *Oliver!* I bought a ticket and went inside. I'd never gone to a play before, and it seemed like a nice warm place to relax for a while. Before I knew it, I was swept up in the show and able to get my mind off my misery. What would it be like to be up there in the lights making people laugh and cry? I wondered.

The next semester I signed up for an acting course. And then another. I loved the classes, from the corny little relaxation exercises to the emotional intensity of scene study. It didn't matter if I was one of twelve squid tentacles in a futuristic college production—I was onstage doing what I now knew I wanted to do for the rest of my life.

I knew the odds were against my making it as an actress, but that night in the chapel had given me a faith I relied on time and again: when I applied for a Master of Fine Arts in theater arts and won a scholarship to Cornell; when I moved to New York City, leaving my suitcase with a pretzel vendor while I got headshots made; when I stuck it out after my one-and-a-half-year contract on the soap opera *Ryan's Hope* ended; and when I moved to Hollywood to work in film and television, winning the role of Marilyn Monroe in the miniseries *Marilyn: The Untold Story*, for which I earned an Emmy nomination.

I had just finished roles in the hit movies *Peggy Sue Got Married* and *Star Trek IV: The Voyage Home* when my dad suddenly passed away of a heart attack. I pressed on with work, taking my mom with me to Yugoslavia, where I was filming another movie. Yugoslavia was lovely before the war, and I felt we were in another, simpler world.

In no time I had fallen in love—with my costar. But I wasn't prepared for the pain when we broke up a short time later. At thirty-six, I had had my share of relationships that didn't work out, but this was different. I thought of how Dad sometimes told me I should settle down. I had always been too busy with my career to worry about it much, but now I found myself wanting a family more than anything.

I returned to Arizona with Mom, both of us still hurting from losing men we'd loved. One evening I went to Mass with my mother, seeking solace. Right before receiving communion, I closed my eyes and again sensed an inarticulate prayer, one that came from a place even deeper than my pain.

Once again I knew that God was telling me to trust. By the time I had returned to my pew the pain was gone. Like before, when I had thought all was lost in college, something wonderful was in store for me. I got called to do a role in the movie *Child's Play*. On the set I kept hearing about the "genius" makeup artist Kevin Yagher, who had designed some of the puppets I had to work with. During filming he shyly approached me a couple of times and complimented my work. At the wrap party we talked for hours. Behind the movie's Chicago skyline backdrop, he kissed me good night softly, and in that moment I knew my prayer had been answered.

Kevin and I got engaged, and I decided to buy a house for Mom on the island of Coronado, near San Diego, where we had spent many happy summers with Dad while I was growing up. I picked out a Cape-Cod-style blue house with white trim and had it furnished. It was so much more than a house to both of us—it was a sanctuary where I could visit her more often than when she lived in Arizona. I was proud to use my success to do something special for Mom.

It seemed like everything had finally worked out. Kevin and I were married in 1990, and our daughter, Catie, was born two years later. But in the meantime, the acting industry had become very youth-driven and I wasn't getting much work. I didn't mind at first because I was able to spend lots of time with my new family and with my mom in Coronado, helping her plant her garden and swimming in the ocean together. But then the house payments started taking their toll. I called my agent daily and I auditioned for parts that I would have scoffed at just a few years earlier. Finally I landed a part on a TV show, but it was soon canceled. I dug into my retirement plan. Since Mom had developed health problems, the house was even more important—I could drive down from L.A. in an emergency. I had to hold onto that house.

I networked when I could and did some guest spots on TV series. I even called the sponsors of a local Star Trek convention to see if I could make some money for appearing, but they only wanted stars from the newer series and movies. After twenty years, my acting career seemed over.

In 1994 my husband and my business manager both confronted me.

"Catherine," my manager said, "you're going to spend every last penny you have if you hold onto that house. You must sell it."

I turned to my husband. "I know how you feel about this, honey," he said, "but there's just no other way." I gazed out the window at the steel-and-glass Los Angeles skyline. Was it all for nothing, Lord? I wondered. All the obstacles I'd overcome, all the leaps of faith I'd taken to build a life I loved, and here I was, once again stuck at a dead end and silently crying out for God's help.

And there he was again, reminding me to trust him. I didn't have to cling to the house, only to him. He would do the rest.

Mom and I agreed she would move back to Arizona while a real estate agent found a buyer. I would make the payments for as long as I could and then let it go. By Easter 1995 the house still had not been sold and my savings were nearly gone. I went out to visit Mom. We were having coffee in the kitchen late one afternoon when my agent called.

"Catherine, Aaron Spelling just called! He offered you a role in a new family-oriented series about a minister and his wife raising five kids."

The show was *7th Heaven*. When I read the script I knew God had worked things out once again. I would be portraying the mother in the kind of close family I'd grown up in. And my own mother wouldn't have to give up the house we both loved. Today Catie and I often watch *7th Heaven* with Mom when we visit her in Coronado.

There have been many happy endings along the way. There have been crises, too, and there will be again; there always are. But maybe it's in the tough times that we really get to know God—when we let go of our ideas of what life should be and discover the better plan God has in mind, better than we could ever have imagined for ourselves.

SILENT TREATMENT

KATHY MATTEA

*Singer Kathy Mattea is a two-time Grammy winner and winner of multiple
Country Music Association and Academy of Country Music awards.*

A had never experienced anything quite like it. Late in 1991 I was performing at a club in London. Near the end of the set, I was singing "You're Not the Only One" when I reached for a high F near the top of my vocal range. What came out, however, didn't sound like me. I felt like a rock climber grabbing a familiar handhold only to have it crumble away.

I made it through the final number and an encore, but as I walked offstage the band gathered around me. Those guys knew my voice inside out. They could tell it had been more than a simple missed note.

My manager rushed backstage. "Are you all right?" he asked, concern tightening his voice.

"I'm fine. Just a little tired." My mind was racing. All singers have ups and downs. No one is one hundred percent every night. You just learn to sing around the problems. My schedule was booked tight, and I had obligations to promoters, audiences, my musicians, and the crew. To stop would mean more pressure than going on. I couldn't quit. I had been on an award-winning streak for three years, and I had waited all my life for the touring opportunities I now had.

I have loved music ever since I can remember. I was a precocious kid, and early on teachers warned my mom to keep me busy so I wouldn't get bored. She threw me into every activity she could think of, and music was the one thing that stuck.

It never bored me; there was always something to learn. I learned piano and guitar, then I started singing.

Eventually I began playing folk Masses at our tiny Catholic church in Nitro, West Virginia, picking guitar and singing solos. We lived in Protestant country. The Baptist church across the street let out halfway through Mass; and I can remember our priest trying to speak over the steeple bells, which were thirty yards from our open church doors. We strained to hear him and tried not to giggle at how comical the situation was. There was something earthy and real in our little church. The music was heartfelt, and everyone sang as loudly as they could. My years there taught me that music is a way to embrace God, and I never doubted where my singing came from.

After two years of studying engineering and physics at West Virginia University, I missed music so much that I decided to move to Nashville. I had always dreamed of a music career, and I prayed for guidance. I didn't care if I became famous; I was in search of a more interesting life. After some rough months, I began a spiritual ritual of putting myself in God's hands every day. I prayed for a path, a niche, and I prayed for clear vision. If I didn't have what it took, I wanted to be able to let go and get on with my life.

I found my path and it had led to the stage in London that night. Exciting things were happening, yet they were coming at me so quickly that I didn't have time to enjoy them. I started feeling the pressure of success, the double-edged sword that it can be. Some mornings I woke up more tired than when I went to bed. When I began to question my feelings, the guilt kicked in. Who was I to complain? How many people would like to be exactly where I was now? Didn't I have everything I ever wanted? Hadn't God put me on my path? I began to wonder if I were having a nervous breakdown.

After the London show I flew back to Nashville. At that point I couldn't even sing. The next morning I saw Dr. Ed Stone at the Vanderbilt Voice Clinic.

"Just relax, Kathy," he said as he passed a fiber-optic instrument attached to a video camera to the back of my throat. I tried to breathe and stay calm. I looked at a monitor. The camera would show my vocal cords, a pair of membranes no thicker than a nickel that produce a miraculous range of sound.

"Say *aah*," the doctor instructed.

"*Aah* . . . "

I saw my epiglottis move and then something truly horrifying. I expected my cords to be raw and red, even a bit swollen; that was par for the course after a long run. But I had never seen anything like this—a large red ball, like a blood blister, directly on top of one of the cords. Instinctively, I pulled back and gasped. Before I could stop myself, I was sobbing.

Doctor Stone let me cry for a while, then he softly encouraged me to let him take a closer look. I wiped my tears and tried to compose myself. "Kathy, you need complete vocal rest," he said. "You must not sing. You must not speak—not a word, not even a whisper. Try not to laugh. You need to rest. Not just your voice but your whole body. Take a little time off. Relax."

After three weeks, the doctors at the Voice Clinic would have another look. We would learn more about our options when they could see my cords without the swelling and inflammation. No one said it, but we were all thinking surgery. I had three weeks of nothing to do but worry about the future.

My manager had come to the clinic, and we discussed canceling all my engagements for two months. He didn't blink an eye. "Done," he said. I drove home and explained the situation to my husband, Jon. That was the last I would talk for twenty-one days.

It was strange taking time off in the middle of summer, usually my heaviest touring season. And it was odder still to be utterly silent. No rehearsals, no meetings, no interviews, no chats with friends. I went from ninety miles an hour to a screeching halt. At first it was uncomfortable, and then I began to feel peaceful. I listened more. I began to realize how much I used my voice to define myself in all aspects of my life. And I had no choice but to sit quietly, alone with myself even in a crowded room.

That day, after my conversation with Jon, I laced on an old pair of running shoes and hit the beautiful walking trails of Radnor Lake, a nature preserve six miles from downtown Nashville. I needed to take some action in order to feel I was contributing to the healing process, and that was my first step.

I started going for long walks every day. As I wandered through the sun-dappled woods on the ridge overlooking the lake, I held silent conversations with myself and listened for answers. At first, the walking gave me comfort—a feeling of getting away from my problems. But as time went on, my physical exercise became spiritual exercise. I thought about my priorities. I thought about the role my work played in my life. I worked hard and I loved it. Still, I felt overwhelmed by success, and at times my life seemed out of control. Where had I gone wrong?

I thought back to simpler times in my life—to West Virginia and our little church. I had found my voice there. It had felt so right to sing. Had I ruined my voice by doing what I thought God wanted me to do? How could I make sense of that? What if I couldn't sing ever again? What if I was never the same? Waves of fear would wash over me, and I'd cry uncontrollably.

During my walks I began to face fear and regarded it as my constant companion. I would visualize it as a small creature who lived on my right shoulder. It looked, in my mind, like a gargoyle. It wasn't going to go away, but I had God on my side. Eventually I became bold enough to talk to it. In my mind I would say, I can't get rid of you, but I am going through this to the other side, and God is going to lead me. I began to realize that I had no idea what God had planned for me. Maybe there was some other path I was supposed to take, and this was his way of getting me there.

I began to see small signs. While waiting for a CAT scan of my neck to check for tumors, I spotted a little girl, about five years old. She was on her dad's lap, and I could see a catheter tube peeking out from under her gown. I looked around the room at an elderly man on a gurney, waiting as I was. He was pale and thin. And I realized that those people had much bigger struggles than I had. My condition was not life-threatening. I would go on, voice or not. I would find the next thing to do. Suddenly I knew it would be okay, that God was indeed taking care of me, in his own way.

As my daily walks continued, I began to realize it was my soul as much as my body that needed healing. I began to see my injury (my "ruby," as I had come to nickname it) as a gift. Nothing else would have gotten my attention in the same way. I surrendered myself completely. And I was truly ready for whatever happened next.

The three weeks of silence passed quickly; and after another three weeks of vocal therapy, I cautiously returned to singing. I began to tour again and even recorded another album. I was living with the injury and doing well until it hemorrhaged about a year later. Surgery became unavoidable at that point. It was a bit of a roller-coaster ride, but I had new reserves and my physical and spiritual rituals to get me through it. I just kept turning everything over to God. He was in control—not me, not my fear, and not even my doctors.

The surgery was a success, and today my voice is stronger than ever. More importantly, my faith is stronger. Like my body, it needs daily exercise. When I do my spiritual calisthenics, life doesn't seem so complicated and stressful. Certainly everything does not always happen the way I want it to. I have setbacks and disappointments. I question as much as I accept. But that's how I grow.

Earlier this year I went through some soul-searching. And for one of the few times in my life I asked God for a concrete answer. I sent up a prayer asking for some confirmation that I was offering something with my singing. I said, "If I'm supposed to quit, just let me know. I'll go on to the next thing if it's time . . ."

That night, while I met fans after the show, a woman was walking away after having her picture taken with me. She stopped, turned around, took hold of my arm, looked me directly in the eye and said, "Don't quit. Your music means so much to us."

It was all I needed to hear.

The Value of Integrity

TRUE COURAGE:
NOW I KNOW WHAT IT MEANS

JOHN WAYNE

John Wayne found great success, including an Oscar for True Grit,
in his many roles in western movies.

ong before I ever made the movie *True Grit*, people would talk about my screen characters in terms of courage, firmness, stamina—true grit. But what about the man who played those characters?

Certainly I have never thought of myself as the timid type. Even as a child I know I had a certain brashness. I remember two incidents in particular when I was a little boy and my family was homesteading in the Mojave Desert. The four of us— my mother, father, younger brother, and I—had come from a little town in Iowa where Dad had been a pharmacist. Due to his health, the doctors had told him he should move west. At first he had thought about going to Montana, but my grandfather wrote and said, "Why not come to California and starve?" We did both.

Dad found some isolated land in Antelope Valley, not close to anything, yet not too far from Lancaster. He built a house for us that was hardly more than a shack; and he tried to grow corn on the land as though we were back in Iowa, which, clearly, we were not. We had a pretty desperate time of it. I was hardly aware of it because I was happy—and especially, I recall, because I had my own horse that I took care of and rode back and forth to school. Her name was Jenny, and I loved her.

One Halloween night out there in the desert, my brother Bob and I had just come to the table when my mom brought out a bowl full of weenies, a special treat since we didn't have meat very often. Just at that moment we all heard an eerie sound.

"*Who-o-o-o. Who-o-o-o-o.*"

It was my dad standing outside the screen door with a sheet over his head, but I thought it was the bogeyman. I grabbed the bowl of weenies and flung it at the apparition. It broke up dad's performance.

As I look back, hurling that bowl of weenies at the bogeyman came as natural to me as a knee jerk. Not too long after that, though, I was asked to do something that required a different kind of courage. My horse Jenny began to get so thin that people in town accused me of not feeding her. Finally the vet told us that for her own good we should destroy her—which was like destroying me. I didn't want to do it, but it had to be done. So it was done.

Those things were way back in my childhood, but years later, in the fall of 1964, I came face to face with a different kind of demand: cancer, the Big C. In October I'd gone down to the Scripps Clinic in La Jolla for my very belated yearly checkup. I knew I'd been coughing a lot more, but I wasn't in any kind of pain.

The doctors kept taking x-rays, and I was getting impatient. When they sent me back for the fourth set of pictures, I said to the radiologist, "What's the deal?"

"Well, it's positive, of course, but beyond—"

"Wait a minute. Positive? What are you telling me?"

"I'm sorry," the doctor said, "didn't you know?"

When I left the clinic that day, I realized I must have a lung operation as fast as possible and that there were a lot of arrangements to make, but for the moment I was dazed. I'd promised Senator Goldwater, who was running for President then, that I would appear at a rally in San Diego, and I headed there. I sat in the back of the audience instead of on the dais. I don't know why. I wasn't trying to escape attention; I think I just wanted to be close to people.

Before the end of the rally, they had hauled me up on the stage and the crowd cheered. I remember thinking how odd it would be if they knew what was happening in my head, that I was standing there a bewildered man in the first flush of fear.

I'm a big man physically and I was lucky to have been born with an unusual amount of strength and stamina. All my life I've been grateful for those physical gifts. They shaped my career. They made it possible for me to play football for the Southern California Trojans, which led directly to my getting a summer job as a prop man with a movie studio; and a bit of muscle wasn't exactly a hindrance for the rest of my career in pictures either. But any dimwitted thug knows that physical strength is not the same as courage. And that night in San Diego, I needed courage.

Obviously there was no bludgeoning one's way out of this one; there was nothing to hurl at the bogeyman. My very helplessness gave me awful twinges of fear. Mark Twain wasn't being humorous when he wrote that, "Courage is resistance to fear, mastery of fear—not absence of fear." If I was going to do battle with cancer bravely, I knew what it was that I had to conquer first.

In this struggle I had a lot of allies—my family and friends, of course. And prayer. I did a lot of praying in those few shaky days before the operation, and this I know: there is a Man Upstairs holding all this world together, including you and me. You cannot believe this, and believe it firmly, without drawing the strength and the courage to master your fears.

The operation was successful, thank God. They cut away a lung, but they left me alive and grateful, and ready to learn something more about adversity. Overcoming trouble can be like skidding in a car on a slippery road. There's the first skid which, if you can control it, you feel pretty relieved about. But there is an after-skid waiting to surprise you from the other direction. My after-skid was getting back in the harness again.

With all that vaunted energy of mine, I was surprised at how much the operation had slowed me down. I began to think about it, and worry. My conscience hurt me because I had been scheduled to make a picture with Dean Martin called *The Sons of Katie Elder*. Everybody had been most considerate about the postponement, but now time was wasting, careers were being interfered with, money was going down the drain. Finally I made up my mind to do the picture, but I had misgivings about myself, about my strength. Those reservations were taken care of by that tremendous old director, Henry Hathaway.

Hathaway had directed me in a number of films, and luckily he had the assignment on *Katie Elder*. It was he, really, who got me going again, though not with tender loving care. That man was merciless. The film was shot on location in Durango, Mexico, which is eight thousand feet above sea level—not the best place for breathing, even with two lungs. It didn't take me long to figure out what Hathaway was up to. He was being deliberately tough on me. He had me getting soaked in the river and jumping out of rigs handcuffed; he always testing me. I was determined not to let him get the best of me.

One evening we had a night shot in which I was supposed to come riding down a street on a horse carrying a rocking chair in one hand, a Bible in the other, and a basket over one arm. I was supposed to stop, dismount, and walk into a girl's domicile. The horse I was riding had never worked at night before and he was fractious and hard to handle. I kept doing the scene over and over, mounting, dismounting, and mounting again with all those encumbrances. Hathaway watched me carefully, but no more carefully than I was watching myself, for I was getting tired. At last when he finally called out, "Print it! Let's go to bed," I knew for sure that not only had I beaten Hathaway at his game, but that I had also won my fight with cancer.

Why had Hathaway chosen to take such a rough tack with me? Why did I let him? Because more than ten years before, he had undergone an operation for cancer far worse than mine. He knew me well. He knew just how far he could push me and he used the courage he had shown in his own recovery to help bring about mine. Nowadays it's one of the rewards for me that I am able to tell people that simply because they have cancer doesn't mean they're at the end of the road.

It is good and it is helpful to have physical strength; but looking back, I am certain that the truest part of true grit is not physical—it's moral. It's making a decision and standing firm in it, whether it's submitting to an operation or putting an ailing pet to sleep. It's doing what must be done. After all, if you think about it, that's the root of all morality, for no moral man can have peace of mind if he leaves undone what he knows he should have done.

BE CAREFUL OF GRAY

WALTER CRONKITE

Walter Cronkite headlined The CBS News with Walter Cronkite *from 1962 to 1981; in 1973, he was voted "the most trusted man in America."*

There came a time when I was growing up in Houston, Texas, that I wanted to own a watch. In fact, I had a particular watch picked out, an Ingersoll on display in our local drugstore. It cost a dollar. Since I had no money, and no prospects for raising a dollar quickly, I asked the druggist if I could take the watch and pay for it little by little. He agreed, and the next day, when my mother happened to come into the store, he casually mentioned the arrangement we'd made.

My mother would have none of it. She was a woman of scrupulous honesty, and, to her, I'd taken advantage of another person's willingness to trust me. She paid the druggist the dollar and hurried home to confront me.

"Don't you see?" she said. "Your intentions are honorable, but even you admit you don't know how you're going to earn the money for that watch. There's no outright dishonesty here, but you're flirting with it. It's one of those risky gray areas, Walter. Be careful of gray—it might be grime."

Then she took the watch and kept it until I earned the money to retrieve it.

Throughout the years since that experience, I've had plenty of reasons to remember my mother's admonition. As a newscaster I've always had to be on guard against gray—a presentation of only half the facts, a story that didn't ring quite true. And there have been such occasions in my personal life as well. One time, for instance, some speculators offered to give me a large parcel of land. There was no suggestion that I talk about their property on the air. They were not being dishonest; they just wanted to be able to say that I owned land in the area that they were trying to promote. But it seemed like a gray area to me. I didn't accept the offer.

I believe that most of the people in this world are honest and want to be honest. But honesty, like all other virtues, requires vigilance. My mother, Helen Lena Cronkite, knew this. This is what she had in mind as she helped me to stay clear of ambiguity—the gray areas that might be grime.

The Dog Next Door

Jimmy Stewart
as told to Richard H. Schneider

Jimmy Stewart's charm and soft-spoken manner in films such as
It's a Wonderful Life *endeared him to audiences across the land.*

When I was about thirteen years old back home in Indiana, Pennsylvania, I had a dog named Bounce. He was just a street dog of indeterminate parentage who had followed me home from school one day. Kind of like an Airedale, but of an orange color, Bounce became my close companion. He'd frolic alongside me when I'd go into the woods to hunt arrowheads, and snore at my feet when I'd build a model airplane. I loved that dog.

Late one summer I had been away to a Boy Scout camp at Two Lick Creek, and when I got home Bounce wasn't there to greet me. When I asked Mother about him, she gently took me inside. "I'm sorry, Jim, but Bounce is gone."

"Did he run away?"

"No, Son, he's dead."

I couldn't believe it. "What happened?" I choked.

"He was killed."

"How?"

Mom looked over to my father. He cleared his throat. "Well, Jim," he said, "Bogy broke his chain, came over and killed Bounce."

I was aghast. Bogy was the next-door neighbors' English bulldog. Normally he was linked by a chain to a wire that stretched about one hundred feet across their backyard.

I was grief-stricken and angry. That night I tossed and turned. The next morning I stepped out to look at the bulldog, hoping to see at least a gash in its speckled hide. But no, there on a heavier chain stood the barrel-chested villain. Every time I saw poor Bounce's empty house, his forlorn blanket, his food dish, I seethed with hatred for the animal that had taken my best friend.

Finally one morning I reached into my closet and pulled out the Remington .22-caliber rifle Dad had given me the past Christmas. I stepped out into our backyard and climbed up into the apple tree. Perched in its upper limbs, I could see the bulldog as he traipsed up and down the length of his wire. With the rifle I followed him in the sights. But every time I got a bead on him, tree foliage got in the way.

Suddenly a gasp sounded from below. "Jim, what are you *doing* up there?"

Mom didn't wait for an answer. Our screen door slammed and I could tell she was on the phone with my father at his hardware store. In a few minutes our Ford clattered into the driveway. Dad climbed out and came over to the apple tree.

"C'mon down, Jim," he said gently. Reluctantly, I put the safety on and let myself down onto the summer-seared grass.

The next morning, Dad, who knew me better than I knew myself, said, "Jim, after you finish school today, I want you to come to the store."

That afternoon I trudged, kicking dust, downtown to Dad's hardware store, figuring he wanted the windows washed or something. He stepped out from behind the counter and led me back to the stockroom. We edged past kegs of nails, coils of garden hose, and rolls of screen wire to a corner. There squatted my hated nemesis, Bogy, tied to a post.

"Now here's the bulldog," Dad said. "This is the easy way to kill him if you still feel that way." He handed me a short-barreled .22-caliber rifle. I glanced at him questioningly. He nodded.

I took the gun, lifted it to my shoulder, and sighted down the black barrel. Bogy, brown eyes regarding me, panted happily, pink tongue peeking from tusked jaws. As I began to squeeze the trigger, a thousand thoughts flashed through my mind while Dad stood silently by. But my mind wasn't silent; all of Dad's teaching about our responsibility to defenseless creatures, fair play, right and wrong, welled up within me. I thought of Mom loving me after I broke her favorite china serving bowl. There were other voices, including our preacher leading us in prayer and asking God to forgive us as we forgave others.

Suddenly the rifle weighed a ton and the sight wavered in my vision. I lowered it and looked up at Dad helplessly. A quiet smile crossed his face and he clasped my shoulder. "I know, Son," he said gently. I realized then: he had never expected me to pull that trigger. In his wise, deep way he let me face my decision on my own. I never did learn how Dad managed to arrange Bogy's presence that afternoon, but I know he had trusted me to make the right choice.

A tremendous relief overwhelmed me as I put down the gun. I knelt down with Dad and helped untie Bogy, who wriggled against us happily, his stub tail wiggling furiously.

That night I slept well for the first time in days. The next morning as I leaped down the back steps, I saw Bogy next door and stopped. Dad ruffled my hair. "Seems you've forgiven him, Son."

I raced off to school. Forgiveness, I found, could be exhilarating.

WHAT I'VE LEARNED
FROM WEARY WILLIE

EMMETT KELLY

*Emmett Kelly's sad clown persona made him the
most celebrated clown of his era.*

hat's the hardest thing in the world to be? I can tell you in one word: yourself—especially if what you are is different from the crowd. But I'll guarantee this: if you can find the courage to be yourself and to be the person God intended you to be, you'll be all right.

Let me tell you how this old clown found out about all this. Back in the Depression days of the 1930s, work in the circus (or anywhere else) was tough to come by, so when I landed a job as a clown with the Sells-Floto Circus in 1933, I was overjoyed. Before then I'd done some trapeze work, but the idea of being a clown had been germinating in my mind for a long time. While performing high above the audience, I'd watched the clowns with secret envy; now I had my chance.

Right away I knew that I had found my niche—clowning was for me. Trying to cheer people up and making wide-eyed kids and their long-faced parents laugh gave me a deep feeling of satisfaction, and that made me want to do a creative job.

Within a few weeks, however, my creativity turned out to be a problem. When I tried to add a few new touches to my act, the head clown gave me a dressing down. "No freelancing, Kelly. Stay in line."

At that time clowns all looked pretty much the same: powder-white faces, silly white wigs, zany Harpo Marx smiles, and baggy white suits with ruffled collars. We had prescribed uniforms and a prescribed routine. Trained monkeys could have done the job. One day I decided I had to do something original or burst.

In my mind's eye I had this picture of a sad-faced, woebegone hobo clown. He didn't jump into being all at once, though; I dreamed him into reality bit by bit.

As a kid, I loved to draw. When I wasn't doing chores for Dad on our farm in Texas County, Missouri, I was off under a tree sketching. Mother encouraged me and persuaded Dad to pay for a correspondence course in cartooning for me. At age twenty I went off to Kansas City to make my mark. Unfortunately, no one had told Kansas City and the art world that I was coming. As a result, I wound up cutting butter in a creamery. What a career! I'd gone from milking Dad's cows in the country to cutting butter in the city.

Eventually, I did get work as a pen-and-ink cartoonist for a film company that made motion picture trailer ads and lantern slides for movie theaters. One of the characters I created was a baggy-pants hobo.

My career took another track when I joined the circus. Still, the joy of creating things never left me, and when I was searching for some innovative way to develop a new type of clown, that old hobo drawing popped into my mind.

Dusting off my pad and pencils, I began trying to draw the hobo I wanted to bring to life. I knew he was a mournful tramp, rather pathetic, with a six-day beard and ragtag clothes. But there was something about him with which everyone could identify—an underdog, down on his luck, but still trying and still hoping that his ship would come in.

To get the character I wanted, I added a bulbous nose, arched eyebrows, and a sad-sack, turned-down smile. I was getting close.

When the circus played in New York, I went to a costume shop looking for a hat. There I found a battered brown one with dirty splotches on it.

"How much for this one?" I asked.

"Gimme a buck," the proprietor answered. (It was the best buy I ever made.) Then I went to a shoemaker and had him construct the biggest, floppiest shoes I could imagine.

Back in the privacy of my own room, I put on the raggedy clothes and makeup. Looking in the mirror, I saw for the first time the character I'd been dreaming about for so long; and as I looked at him, his name came to me. "Willie. Weary Willie," I said, and now everything was ready for his debut.

The circus moved west and I waited, trying to work up courage to introduce Willie. Finally, in Mason City, Iowa, I donned the clothing and waited until all the others in Clown Alley had entered the Big Top. I followed and it was love at first sight. The audience took one look at Weary Willie and they loved him.

Only the clown master was unsmiling. Afterward he told me to forget the hobo—"too grubby, too scruffy for the circus." So begrudgingly I went back to my all-white costume and finished out the year. But something kept whispering, "Be yourself, Kelly. Don't be like that fellow in the Bible who buried his talent in the ground." When we struck our tents in the last town, I gave notice I was quitting.

It was a big decision. I had a wife and a new son to support; and there was no guarantee I could find another job, but I knew I had to try.

You see, I believed in my Weary Willie creation with all my heart; and when you really believe in something, you are filled with a faith that can move mountains, just like it says in the Bible. The Lord made each of us unique, I believe, and we are truest to him when we are true to ourselves. Anyway, that was the conviction I had about Willie and my future.

A few weeks later I heard about a job opening and went for an interview.

"Well, show me your act," the boss said.

So I put on my costume and makeup and introduced him to Willie. Willie didn't have his whole act together yet. There was no sledgehammer to crack peanuts with and no broom to sweep up the circle of lights made on the floor by a spotlight, but otherwise he was complete.

The circus boss sat through my routine poker-faced, and my heart was right down in my floppy shoes. Finally, when I was through, he shook his head resignedly and laughed out loud.

"I never saw an act like this one," he said, "but I think they'll like you."

He was right. Forty-five years later people still seemed to enjoy Willie's unorthodox antics.

So if you ever worry about being different from the crowd, stop worrying. Weary Willie has had almost half a century of fun just being himself. And so have I.

THE SCARY SEASON

HERSCHEL WALKER

*Herschel Walker won college football's Heisman Trophy in 1982;
he was voted into the College Football Hall of Fame in 1999.*

Football. In Georgia, fall means football. It seems that everyone is a football fan and that every team is someone's favorite. In Athens, sixty thousand students, parents, alumni, and other fans will pack the University of Georgia's Sanford Stadium, wearing red and whooping and hollering for their Georgia Bulldogs.

I was the Bulldogs' running back in 1982, and I could only hope at the beginning of the season that, win or lose, 1982 would not be like our previous season.

It's not as though our record in 1981 was bad—we won ten games and lost only two. For the second straight year, we were Southeastern Conference Champions and ranked among the top ten teams in the country. No, it wasn't the wins or losses at all that made the 1981 season so memorable. It was the way I nearly quit being a part of autumn in Georgia.

On the first day of football practice in the fall, the Georgia Bulldogs were the toast of the state. We'd gone through the 1980 season undefeated and had beaten Notre Dame in the Sugar Bowl, 17–10. Everywhere in Georgia, bumper stickers and T-shirts and frisbees proclaimed the rallying cry of the previous season—"How 'bout them Dawgs?" We had won our last thirteen games in a row, and hardly a fan could be found who didn't think we'd win another twelve in a row and the national championship again.

It had been a good year for me too. I had run for more yards than any freshman in the history of college football and had finished as a runner-up for the prestigious Heisman Trophy, given each year to the nation's best college football player. I was just thankful that God had given me a gift—a strong body and a strong mind—and a chance to use that gift as best I could. Just being at the state university was special for me; it was an opportunity Mama and Daddy had only dreamed of for any of their seven children. But even as practice began, I could sense that that wasn't enough anymore. The previous year was good, so this year would have to be better. For all our fans, nothing else would do.

I was in line to register for classes with the other students a few days before our first game when someone I didn't even know patted me on the back. "We can't lose this year!" he stated emphatically to his buddy as he turned to me. "Not with ol' Herschel out there for us." I suppose it was intended as a compliment, but the comment left me strangely uneasy. The responsibility that was being heaped on my shoulders scared me.

Out on the field, with a football tucked under my arm, I just tried to do what I did best—run toward the goal line. We beat Tennessee the first weekend of the season, 44–0, an outstanding team performance. The bell on top of the campus chapel rang out fourteen times to celebrate our fourteen-game winning streak, now the longest in college football.

It rang fifteen times the next week, after we struggled to a 27–13 win over California. I gained 167 yards rushing, but had fumbled once, just part of a team effort not quite up to par.

That's when the whispering started. It was isolated at first, a few inquiring people wondering if anything was wrong. Why hadn't I broken a long touchdown run yet? Was I worried that my play might jeopardize the winning streak? I was more confused, really. I had gained 328 yards in two wins. Was that so bad?

Coach Vince Dooley worked us hard as we prepared for the third game of the season against Clemson University. This year the game, one of the fiercest college rivalries in the South, would be in Clemson's Memorial Stadium, nicknamed "Death Valley" because of the difficulty opposing teams have winning there. Still, we were favored to win.

We won the coin toss, received the kickoff, and began moving the ball up the field. I picked up eight yards running around left end, another four slashing right. A pass play netted us another first down, and I carried twice more.

On second down, from the Clemson thirteen-yard line, I took a pitchout and headed left. Just as I was about to cut upfield toward the goal line, a Clemson lineman hit my arm. The ball squirted loose, and a pile of orange jerseys were immediately on top of it. I'd just fumbled away a good scoring opportunity.

I fumbled again in the second quarter to set up a Clemson field goal, but by that time our whole team had begun to unravel. Perhaps it was the noisy Clemson fans or maybe it was just a bad day, but nine times that afternoon we lost the ball on fumbles or interceptions. We lost the game, too, 13–3. The bell would not ring that night on the University of Georgia campus.

The locker room was somber as I shuffled in. Reporters surrounded us, probing for reasons for the loss. Herschel, what's wrong? Why aren't you playing like last year? Herschel, are you still happy at Georgia?

The Clemson defeat and the questions dogged me into the next week. No matter how hard I tried, I couldn't avoid it. One afternoon, as I walked to practice, two guys stopped me. "Hey, Herschel, how come you're not running like last year?" I shrugged, mumbled something about doing my best, and walked on. Though I had scored only one touchdown, compared to the five I'd scored after three games last season, I'd run for more yards. Yet, instead of "How 'bout them Dawgs?" everyone seemed to be asking, "What's wrong with Herschel?"

I walked on beneath the campus trees, thinking of the criticisms that had threaded their way in from every corner of Georgia and beginning to believe them myself. Maybe I have lost it, I thought. I'd even heard of bumper stickers that read "Herschel who?" The criticisms and doubts hurt, more than I cared to admit.

I dragged through practice halfheartedly, my mind focused more on what I would tell Coach Dooley than on how to run against South Carolina, our next opponent. I'd decided it might be easier to just quit, to forget the pressure and questions, and the pain that came when your best effort wasn't good enough.

I also decided to wait until the next morning to say anything about quitting. As I dragged myself back to my room that night, I'd never felt so low and alone. Inside I flipped on a small light and flopped down on my bed. "It's not fair," I said out loud. "Why is everybody on my case? Why can't I just be me?"

That's when I caught a glimpse of it out of the corner of my eye—the picture I had hanging over my bed, a picture of Jesus. It somehow looked different this time. As I stared into Christ's face, I couldn't help but think of the stories of His life I'd learned back in Sunday school in Wrightsville, Georgia.

Maybe it was the recollection of those Bible stories that helped me realize what was different. In Jesus' face I saw for the first time an enormous courage. I saw a courage born in his forty-day struggle in the wilderness, and tested day in and day out by people who laughed at him and threatened to arrest him or stone him. I saw the courage he showed on that final night in Gethsemane, when terrible agony forced huge drops of blood from his brow. In Jesus' face was the courage of one who kept on going no matter what the hardship. There was no quitter in that picture.

For the longest time I just looked, drawing strength from the picture. And when

I thought again about why I needed that strength, I realized I'd found the example I needed to follow. Whether the criticisms of me had been fair or not didn't matter—Herschel Walker would be no quitter either.

I was the first one at practice the next day, attentively listening to the coaches' instructions. On the field, I ran with reckless abandon. No, the questions wouldn't stop, and the Clemson game would continue to be talked about. The fans were still expecting a lot from me. But I knew now how to cope with the pressure. By standing up to it, just as Jesus had, and not running from it. I had a job to do!

That Saturday we defeated South Carolina, 24–0; I gained 176 yards and scored two touchdowns. We didn't lose again in the regular season; we won the conference title and were ranked second—behind Clemson.

At the beginning of the 1982 football season, expectations ran high. I was determined to make it my best ever, because of what I learned in 1981: that no matter what job you do, there's someone who understands the pressure and responsibilities you face; who's been through it himself. Jesus will give you the strength and courage to keep going. Look for him. And you'll see it too.

THE QUESTION THAT LIGHTS MY LIFE

PAT BOONE

*Pat Boone's career includes work as a recording artist, film and
television actor, author, entrepreneur, and philanthropist.*

henever I mention that I go to church during the week
and twice on Sundays, and even preach at times if I'm
asked to, it always seems to come out as if I'm some sort of a goody-goody.
Or as if I say it because it would help my career.

Neither is true.

What I do and what I believe are derived from these people: my mother, a registered nurse, and my father, a building contractor in Nashville, Tennessee. They were
steady, decent, believing, basic people, who gave their four children a steady, decent,
believing, basic outlook.

When we were kids we didn't have a car. So we'd drive to church in my father's
little pickup truck. He was a deacon and Sunday school teacher at the church. We
always looked kind of funny pulling up in front of the church in a truck with
"Boone Construction Co." painted on it. But such things brought us all closer
together. We always did things as a family, the six of us, playing or praying.

I have a kind of second father too: Mack Craig. When I first met Mack, he was
the principal of David Lipscomb High School in Nashville, as well as a teacher then
working for his Ph.D. He had his own family to take care of too. He was skinny as a
rail, mostly because he seldom took time to eat; he was always moving at a fast trot
to keep everyone around him happy.

Whenever I was worried about something or had a decision to make, I'd take a walk with Mack or call at his house or even wake him at the most awful hours. And he'd always say: "Forget what it means to you personally, or what you can gain by it or have to give up for it, or what someone else might think of it. Just ask yourself: 'Is it right?' "

Since we met, I have always tried to apply that yardstick to whatever I do.

It isn't always easy—like the question of joining a high school fraternity. To presume an air of exclusiveness, some frats discriminated against boys because of their poverty or beliefs or race. My parents disapproved of that, but when I pledged, intending to join a fraternity, they didn't try to stop me. Something else did: the question that has come to light my life when facing any perplexity. "Is it right?"

When you look at life from that perspective, the decision isn't hard, and you always feel relieved.

Singing was one of those things.

If the truth would be known, it was really my appetite that got me into singing. Starting when I was about ten, my mother used to take me to sing at prayer meetings and other services. Then the ladies asked me to sing at their luncheons and club socials. They wanted free entertainment and I wanted a free meal. They told their husbands about it, and pretty soon I was singing—and eating—at Kiwanis and Rotary too.

Then came the opportunity to sing with a good, local dance band, something I'd never done before. But singing with a dance band meant late hours and being around drinking. Troubled, I got Mack Craig out of bed at some horrible hour in the morning, and we talked about it.

Mack said, "Suppose there are temptations. Of course there will be in singing, as in everything. But there's nothing wrong with being a singer if you handle yourself properly."

Instead of the dance band job, Mack helped get me my first radio show: "Youth on Parade," at the local station. It featured high school kids. I was the master of ceremonies and sang a little too. We did it for two years, my senior year in high school and freshman year in college. There was no pay at all, but it was great.

While in college I married Shirley Foley, a wonderful girl. She's the daughter of Red Foley, the TV star of *Country Music Jubilee*; and Shirley and I were high school sweethearts. We both transferred to North Texas State College in Denton, Texas; with marriage, eating became a definite challenge. I needed a real paying job. I got one as a TV entertainer in Fort Worth, and I continued in college.

Following an appearance on *Ted Mack's Original Amateur Hour*, Randy Wood, the president of Dot Records, asked me to come to Chicago to make a recording of "Two Hearts." I hesitated a little. If the impossible happened—a hit record—everything might go haywire. I was making $44.50 a week on TV and radio, which wasn't much, but it was enough to pay our way. Besides, our first daughter, Cheryl Lynn, was already here and our second, Linda Lee, was on the way.

Was it right to leave the security my family had then on the slim chance of a hit record? And what about my schooling?

My father and Shirley felt I should take that chance—so did Mack Craig. Shirley said she was sure I'd finish school whether the record was a hit or not.

It was. And then I was asked to move to New York. That was a much bigger step than Chicago. But I could attend Columbia, something I wanted to do. Everything seemed to fall into place when Arthur Godfrey invited me to be on his show any time school permitted.

Then came the offer to make a movie, *Bernadine*. The picture was to start in January, which meant I would have had to drop out of school before the term ended.

That presented a problem. A lot of kids I know, and a lot of others who wrote me, said that if I could work and go to school full-time, they could too. But if I dropped out before the term ended just for money, wouldn't I be letting them down? The movie people said it would cost an awful lot of money to postpone the picture. What was right?

I finished the term, but agreed to skip the following term to make the movie, which meant graduating in January instead of in June.

We all usually know what wrong is. I'm not sure we all know as often what right is. Mostly right is determined for me by what the Bible says and by how my parents and Mack Craig and other people I admire and respect live by it.

Like them, I always ask myself about anything I do: Will it violate my conscience? Will it have a bad effect on others? Will it have a good effect on others?

I'm not always sure about these things, but I try to be.

My co-managers, Jack Spina and Randy Wood, also asked these questions about any place I was requested to perform or any song I was asked to sing. Sometimes it cost us.

When once we were offered a song to record called "Roll With Me Henry," we all knew it was going to be a sure hit. But the lyrics seemed suggestive. So we didn't record it. Another singer did, under a different title and with changed lyrics, and it sold over a million records.

Before we got the TV show we liked, we were offered many. One came from a cigarette sponsor. I don't smoke, and it would be hypocrisy to ask others, especially teenagers, to smoke. I couldn't feel honest about it. So I asked the sponsor: "Suppose I went before the camera and said, 'I don't smoke. I don't advise you to smoke, but if you're going to smoke, smoke this brand.'"

They laughed and then said, "Why, that's a new approach. Maybe we ought to try it."

They were getting serious, so we cut it off quickly.

What all this means is that we should try to act the way we believe, publicly as well as privately.

No matter how long my singing career lasts, it's given me a great responsibility, and not just to my family, but to the many who look to singers as their example. I owe these fans a lot, if not everything. The only way I can repay them is to make a day-to-day reality of the question that lights my life: "Is it right?"

A NICE FELLOW FROM A SMALL TOWN

HUGH DOWNS

Hugh Downs worked in the field of broadcast journalism for more than
fifty years, most recently in the role of co-anchor of ABC News' 20/20.

ecently, I retired from a long career as a broadcast journalist. My last job was with ABC Television on *20/20*, but before that I had been Jack Paar's sidekick on the original *Tonight Show* and hosted the game show *Concentration*. And of course there were all those early, early mornings when I hosted *Today*. According to the *Guinness Book of World Records*, by 1986 I had logged over 10,000 hours of airtime on national television. Evidently, that's a record.

I wouldn't have survived for one hour were it not for some good advice I received right at the start. I was all of eighteen years old and working at WLOK Radio in Lima, Ohio. I had had to drop out of college because of my father's business setbacks. Dad's partner declared bankruptcy, but Dad was determined to pay back all their creditors. And that meant no more school for me.

Even though WLOK was just a 100-watt, small-town radio station, I was determined to sound like the big time. Leaning into the huge microphone, I focused on speaking in "pear-shaped tones," desperate to find a cool, sophisticated persona. But for all my attempts not to be mistaken for a hick, I left no doubt that I was an amateur. I sounded like what I was: some kid trying to act like he wasn't one.

Finally the program director took me aside. "Forget your voice," he said. "Just remember who you are—a nice fellow from a small town in Ohio."

That advice worked like a charm. My persona was *me*. It was just what I needed then, and later in New York, on the *Tonight Show* and *Today*. Sure, there would be times when I'd suffer a moment of self-consciousness with a famous guest or a big story. Just be who you are, I would remind myself. Just be who God made you. It always worked.

These days in retirement, I'm working on a few Internet ideas. A whole new world is out there on the Web. And it can be a little intimidating too. But sixty-one years after WLOK and more than 10,000 hours of airtime later, I still remind myself: I'm just an ordinary guy from a small town in Ohio.

The
Kindness of
Others

STRANGERS ON THE ROAD

LLOYD BRIDGES

Lloyd Bridges performed in more than 150 films throughout his career;
two of his four children, Jeff and Beau, followed in his acting footsteps.

My wife, Dorothy, and I often enjoy the company of our grandchildren at breakfast in our sunny kitchen in Los Angeles. And when they're with us they take part in our regular morning devotions, as did their parents before them. The other morning as Dotty was reading aloud the parable of the Good Samaritan, I saw a little hand tentatively reach for a sugared doughnut. At that moment I caught myself wondering just how much children remember of the things we read and teach them. Do seeds really sprout and take root in their minds, and influence their lives?

Later, I was thinking about the parable Dotty read that morning and my mind drifted back to a day when I was a traveler on my own road to Jericho. Only it was near Eureka, California, on a rainy Christmas morning over forty years ago.

I remember how the sleet slashed at our windshield as I drove our old Dodge sedan down a twisting wilderness road along the Eel River. There were six of us crowded in that car—Dotty and me, our three-year-old son Beau, my sister, and her two small children. We were on our way to spend Christmas with my mother.

As we nosed down a steep curve, my brakes suddenly gave out and we began to slide out of control. "Hold on!" I yelled to the others as I steered the car into the metal guardrail where, thank God, the car lurched to a stop.

After making sure that we were all safe, I tried to back the car on to the road. I felt that if I could drive in low gear I'd have enough control to make it to a repair garage. But on shifting into reverse, the car wouldn't budge. The front bumper was locked into the guardrail.

For a moment I sat silent, the rain drumming on the metal roof above us.

"Lloyd, what can we do?" asked Dotty.

"I don't know," I sighed. "But we can't stay in the car." Other autos occasionally splashed around us and I feared that in the mist we might not be seen and some car might crash into us, toppling us into the river below.

The cold rain soaked us all as we climbed out. The rest of the family huddled under a tree while I tried to pry the bumper loose from the guardrail with a tire iron. But it was in vain.

My only hope was to flag a ride to a garage and get a tow truck.

Squinting into the rain, I stepped out and waved at a passing car. It veered and disappeared around the curve. Hunched in my soggy coat collar, I waved at car after car. But all of them swished past, with only the faces of the little children peering curiously out the back windows at me. I realized how dangerous it would be for anyone to stop on that hairpin turn. Who would want to jeopardize his life for a stranger?

In despair, I was about to begin slogging down the road when a car slowed, made a U-turn, and came back to me. The driver rolled down a fogged window.

"What's wrong?" he asked. From their clothes, it was obvious that he, his wife, and little girl were dressed up for Christmas or church—or both.

"My car is locked into the guardrail," I said, "and I need a lift to a garage."

He studied his steering wheel for a moment, said something to his wife, and climbed out into the rain.

"No, please." I urged. "You're getting all wet."

"That's okay," he said, sloshing to the guardrail. After examining it, he went to his trunk and pulled out giant cutting shears. "I'm a tinsmith," he said. "Maybe these will help."

I followed him back to my car, feeling terribly guilty as his good dark blue suit got soaked. Grunting with effort, he slowly cut the heavy metal with the powerful shears. As he cut through the last of the rail, the bumper popped free.

"There," he exhaled, stepping back.

"Thank you, thank you!" I exclaimed, reaching for my wallet.

He waved it away and climbed back into his car. "Hey," he said, "you needed help. I was glad to give it. After all, we're all brothers, aren't we?" Putting his car in gear, he called out the window, "Merry Christmas!" and drove away.

"Merry Christmas, and God bless you," I echoed quietly, as I watched his tail-lights disappear into the mist.

Many years later, on a crisp fall evening, Dotty and I were in New York on business, during the days when I was playing the part of Mike Nelson the skin diver and adventurer in the television series, *Sea Hunt*. That evening we were window-shopping our way across town.

As we neared Sixth Avenue, we noticed a commotion taking place on the next corner. An excited crowd stood watching something at the intersection.

I was appalled to see what was going on. A large man, obviously drunk and in a rage, was hurling huge chunks of concrete and other rubble from a construction site into the street. Roaring foul language, he narrowly missed the cars passing by.

A woman was pleading from a nearby parked car: "Somebody help my husband! He doesn't know what he's doing!"

It was obvious that before the police could arrive someone could be terribly hurt. There were exclamations and a snicker here and there among the onlookers, but no one was doing anything. Yet it was understandable. Who would want to reason with a madman?

I was about to suggest to Dotty that we go the other way when it seemed that out of the distant past I heard those words again. *Hey, we're all brothers, aren't we?* Suddenly, over Dotty's anguished protests, I found myself stepping forward through the crowd to the enraged man. Grasping his powerful shoulders under a sweat-dampened blue suit, I pleaded: "Come on, your wife is calling you."

He twisted free and lunged for another chunk of concrete.

I grabbed his arm. "You don't want to hurt someone, or hurt yourself."

With an angry roar, he swung around to face me, and then his jaw dropped. Staring at me wide-eyed, he exclaimed, "Mike Nelson!"

"Yeah," I said, gently guiding him, "let's go to your car."

But he was already a step ahead of me. Pulling me to his wife, he exclaimed, "Look, honey, I found Mike Nelson. Mike Nelson is here!"

The rage had left him and soon he was slumped in the backseat where he promptly fell asleep.

His wife looked up through tear-filled eyes. "He's a good man, but tonight he was badly insulted by someone and he started drinking to try to escape his hurt. He was so angry he just seemed to lose his mind. I don't know how to thank you."

She reached through the driver's window and grasped my hand. "God bless you," she said, then drove off.

As I watched the car's taillights disappear into the night, I remembered that rainy morning on the road by the Eel River and thought about seeds being planted.

And so at our breakfast table as I listen with the little ones to the old, old stories, I pray that Jesus' words will fall on good soil, to be held fast in honest and good hearts, and bring forth much fruit (Luke 8:15, KJV).

THE SECRET BEHIND MY SUCCESS

CAROL BURNETT

*Carol Burnett's much-loved variety show ran for eleven years
and garnered more than twenty Emmy awards.*

My career—TV, stage, movies, all of it—was founded on a strange event that was to be a deep mystery to me for years. Only after my life had changed drastically, did I begin to solve the puzzle I was confronted with one long-ago June evening in California.

In those days I was one of a group of stage-struck drama school students at UCLA, living on hopes and dreams and not much else. As school ended, one of our professors was leaving for a vacation in Europe. He had a house near San Diego, and a bon voyage party was planned. It was suggested that some of us drama students might drive down and entertain his supper guests with scenes from musical comedies.

Nine of us agreed to go. One of the boys and I had rehearsed a scene from *Annie Get Your Gun*, I remember, and that was our part of the program. Everything went well. The guests seemed to enjoy our singing, and we enjoyed it too.

After our performance, supper was announced. I was standing at the buffet when a man I had never seen before spoke to me pleasantly. He said he had admired our performance. Then he asked me what I intended to do with my life.

I told him that I hoped to go to New York some day and make a career for myself on the stage. When he asked what was stopping me, I told him truthfully that I barely had enough money to get back to Los Angeles, let alone New York. I might have added, but didn't, that at times my grandmother, my mother, my sister and I had been on welfare. The man smiled and said that he would be happy to lend me the money to go to New York. A thousand dollars, he added, should be enough to get me started.

Well, in those days I was pretty innocent, but not that innocent. So I refused his offer politely. He went away, but in a few moments he was back with a pleasant-faced lady whom he introduced as his wife. Then he made his offer all over again. He was quite serious, he said. There were only three conditions. First, if I did meet with success, I was to repay the loan without interest in five years. Next, I was never to reveal his identity to anyone. Finally, if I accepted his offer, I was eventually to pass the kindness along, to help some other person in similar circumstances when I was able to do so.

He told me to think it over and telephone him when I got back to Los Angeles. He added that he was prepared to make a similar offer to my partner in the scene from *Annie Get Your Gun*, and he gave me his telephone number.

The next day, half-convinced I had dreamed the whole thing, I called the number. I was told that if I had decided to accept the conditions, I could drive down on Monday morning and pick up my check. Still unbelieving, I told my mother and grandmother. Their reaction, not surprisingly, was to urge me strongly not to have anything to do with my mysterious benefactor. But somehow I was convinced that the man was sincere, and I believed, furthermore, that the good Lord was giving me, Carol Burnett, a strong and unmistakable push. I was *supposed* to accept the offer. I was being guided. And if I didn't go, I would regret it for the rest of my life.

At sunup on Monday morning my partner and I were on the road. We drove for three hours. At nine o'clock, we were at the man's office. We had to wait perhaps half an hour—and believe me, that was the longest half-hour of my life! But finally we were ushered in. Our friend was crisp, serious, businesslike. He reminded us of the conditions, especially the one about not revealing his identity. Then he had his secretary bring in the checks. I watched as he signed them. I had never seen so many beautiful zeros in my life.

We tried to thank him, but he just smiled and ushered us out. When we came to the car, still dazed, we realized we didn't have enough gasoline to get back to Los Angeles—and not enough cash to buy any. We had to go to a bank, present one of the thousand-dollar checks, then wait while the astonished bank officials telephoned our friend's office to make sure that we weren't a pair of international forgers. But finally they did cash it for us.

Back in Los Angeles, I wasted no time. I spent a little of the money on a visit to the dentist where I had two teeth filled and one extracted—I hadn't been able to afford a dentist for years. Then, with my family's anxious admonitions ringing in my ears, I headed for New York.

In all of that vast city I knew just one soul, a girl named Eleanore Ebe. I called her up and found that she was staying at the Rehearsal Club, where in those days young theatrical hopefuls could find room and board for eighteen dollars a week. So I moved in with Ellie and settled down to the long grind of finding work on the New York stage.

It was the old story. No experience? Then no work. But how can you get experience if you can't get work? My funds got lower and lower. I went to work as a hatcheck girl in a restaurant. Unfortunately, it catered mostly to ladies who had no desire or reason to check their hats. Still, I managed to make about thirty dollars a week from tips—enough to get by.

My grandmother wrote me sternly that if I hadn't found a job on the stage by Christmas I had better come home. So I redoubled my visits to theatrical agencies. Finally one agent said wearily, "Why don't you put on your own show? Maybe then you'd stop bothering us!"

That sparked an idea. Back at the Rehearsal Club I talked to all my jobless friends. If we were really bursting with talent, as we were sure we were, why not hire a hall, send out invitations to all the agents and critics in town, and put on our own revue?

Everyone agreed that it was a great idea. We started chipping in fifty cents apiece each night for a fund to hire the hall. Talented youngsters took on the task of creating scenery, writing music and lyrics, doing the choreography. When our first act was ready, we performed it for the board of directors of the Club who then gave us some additional help. When the "Rehearsal Club Revue" finally opened and ran for three nights, it seemed to us that everyone in New York show business was in the audience. The day after it closed, three agents called me with offers of jobs. From that point on, the magic doors swung open and I was on my way.

I reported all my progress to my benefactor back on the West Coast, but I heard very little from him. He continued to insist upon his anonymity. He showed no desire to share any spotlights, take any credit.

Five years to the day after I accepted his loan, I paid him back, and since then I've kept my pledge never to reveal his identity. He never told me his reasons for helping me in the manner he did; but as the years have gone by, I've been able to unravel the mystery of this man, at least to my own satisfaction and in the process, I've discovered a powerful spiritual principle to use in my own life.

I stumbled upon the key clue one day when I was glancing through a copy of the Living Bible. I had turned to Matthew 6 because I wanted to see how the Lord's Prayer had been translated. Suddenly, some other verses seemed to leap out of the page: "When you give a gift to a beggar, don't shout about it as the hypocrites do . . .

When you do a kindness to someone, do it secretly . . . And your Father who knows all secrets will reward you . . ." (Matthew 6:2–4, TLB).

Do it secretly, the passage read, and at once I thought of my secretive friend. From that moment, what he had done and how he had done it began to make sense.

I began to see that when he made his offer to me, my benefactor had employed the spiritual principle of giving in secret without seeking credit. He had done it partly to be kind, of course, but also because he knew that great dividends flow back to anyone who is wise enough to practice this kind of giving.

I believe that, as the Bible says, there is a great liberating force in not trying to take credit for one's good deeds. It tames the ego. It moves us away from petty vanity— and I'm convinced that the further we move away from ourselves, the closer we come to God.

So that's the story of how my career began. I shall always be grateful to my anonymous friend. With pride I repaid his loan, and with pride I have kept his name secret. As for his stipulation about passing the kindness along to others—well, that's my secret!

THE BIG SLUMP

SAL BANDO

*Sal Bando played third base for the Oakland A's from 1968 to 1981;
during that time, the A's won five division titles and three World Series.*

Ou know what a slump is, don't you? It happens in everyone's life: You hit a period when nothing is going right, and no matter how hard you try, you can't seem to pull out of it.

Bad as it is for some people, it's worse for us ballplayers. Our livelihood rides on what we do out on the field. And when we're failing in game after game, it's not a private hell but a public one, with thousands of people looking on. It's one of the most frightening things that can happen to a player.

I know, because it happened to me in 1975. I went from being one of the top players on the Oakland A's (always the guy who could produce the home runs and RBIs) to nothing. My fielding was terrible, my batting was worse—and I had been one of the best clutch hitters in the game. It was eating me up inside, particularly after I read in a newspaper that the A's owner, Charlie Finley, told reporters I was the worst third baseman in the American League.

Just like an executive who's having problems at the office, the disastrous slide in my career began to affect my home life. I neglected my wife, Sandra, and our two boys. I became moody and withdrawn. When I wasn't trying to figure out what was wrong with my batting stance, I'd be worrying about an important upcoming game.

"What's wrong, honey?" Sandra would ask.

"Nothing," I'd reply.

"Sal, maybe you're trying too hard."

With that I'd stomp out of the room.

We weren't at the battling stage yet, but our marriage was showing the strain in a hundred little ways. And that only put added pressure on me. It was a vicious, descending spiral of worry and frustration.

Another thing that was bugging me was our manager, Alvin Dark. Dark was a peculiar guy. He'd been manager of the A's when I was a rookie, back in the '60s. He was short-tempered and always in hot water with the team's management. Dark left the team after a dispute, but by the time he was rehired in 1974, he had changed.

Dark and his wife, Jackie, had become born-again Christians. The difference in him was unbelievable. There were no more temper tantrums, and he actually talked about God, faith, and love on the baseball field and in the locker room. Reporters began describing Dark as the "ministerial manager" and "goody two-shoes."

Nobody ridiculed him more mercilessly than my teammates and I. We laughed at the way he walked, the way he talked, the fact that he had no vices. But the worst thing was his meekness: How could a manager not fight with the front office or chew us guys out? The man wasn't human. I kept watching to see if he'd blow his cool, but he never did. Alvin Dark was a real pain in the neck to me, but under his management we won the 1974 World Series!

My troubles began the next year. Maybe losing out in a salary arbitration with management triggered it, but I went into my slump. Dark tried to help me. I would listen to him politely, and then do things my way. We were on different wavelengths. Still, everything might have gone up in smoke that year if it hadn't been for Dark's persistence.

It began in a very upsetting way. In mid-season, Dark moved me from number one in the batting lineup to eighth. As team captain and a very prideful guy, I was angered by the insult. When Dark tried to explain why he had to move me, and added that he was praying for me, it was salt in the wound. My lighthearted mockery of his faith hardened into near-hatred.

Things came to a head in June when I returned from a road trip and Sandra greeted me with some incredible news: She had committed her life to Christ.

I just stared at her. We were Roman Catholics and churchgoers. "I know you can't understand it now, honey," she said quietly, "but Jackie Dark lent me a wonderful book. You really ought to read it . . ."

"Jackie Dark! I might have known it!" I exploded. "Sandy, we don't need that born-again stuff! We don't kill; we don't steal; we believe in God!"

"That's not enough, Sal," she replied. Her lower lip trembled.

The nerve of that guy! I thought. When he couldn't get to me directly, he used his wife and Sandra! But Sandra insisted it was not that way; she had been friends with Jackie for a long time. The Darks were only trying to help—and we certainly needed help.

For a couple of days I was really irked. Then I began to see a difference in Sandra. She was more patient with the boys, and even my moodiness didn't seem to faze her. She had the same calm, unflappable quality I had observed in Alvin Dark. It was a stark contrast to my own confusion and unhappiness. And it set me to thinking.

In July, Sandra took the boys home to visit her parents in New Jersey. I had a day to kill before going to Boston for a game, and rattled around the empty house feeling lonely and depressed. Before turning in, I showered, then settled down in bed with a magazine. A book on the night table caught my eye. *His Stubborn Love,* the jacket read. It was the book, by Joyce Landorf, that Sandra had been talking about. My curiosity was piqued. Might as well see what it's all about, I thought, idly picking it up.

There weren't any fireworks, but as I read, I began to understand what it really meant to commit your life to Jesus Christ, as opposed to simply believing in him in a lukewarm way.

When I finished, I lay there a long time, staring at the ceiling. My magazine had fallen, unopened, to the floor.

Finally, throwing back the covers, I slipped out of bed onto my knees. In simple terms, I asked Christ to take over my life. "Please come close, Lord; be real to me. Forgive me for not loving you, for having forgotten you . . ."

At Boston the next night, I surprised myself by getting two hits, including a single to right field that brought in the winning run. After that game I went from ice-cold to being the hottest hitter on the team.

There were other changes: I found myself more conscious of my attitudes and actions toward other people. For one thing, I began making more time for my family. Sandra and I went to a Marriage Encounter group, and it helped our relationship tremendously. In the clubhouse and on the ball field, I began to share with the other players, particularly the younger guys. They had problems, too, and a few encouraging words helped. I began participating in the Sunday baseball chapel programs, sharing my faith.

In the final weeks of the season, my batting average went up from .190 to .230. I doubled my home-run production, ending up with a respectable fifteen for the season. I played some part in getting the A's into the league playoffs. These were not terrific accomplishments on the face of them, but they were to a guy who'd been in the cellar.

What had happened? There's really nothing magical or mysterious about it. I had been tied up in knots all season, worrying about my performance, worrying about what people thought of me, worrying about *myself*. By giving my life over to Jesus, I began caring about other people and reaching *out* instead of *in*; I began to loosen up and automatically began to play better.

I had learned Alvin Dark's secret: The reason he didn't fight with the front office or scream at the players was that he wasn't overly concerned about himself or his position. His Christian faith had made him a selfless, caring person—he cared about the team, he cared about Sal Bando . . .

I'm convinced that the way to get out of a slump, whether it's on the baseball field or in the office, the classroom or the kitchen, is to stop worrying so much about yourself and your own problems. Direct your attention upward, to God, and then outward, to helping others. Be a caring person.

Saint Paul put it just right when he said, "Each of you must regard, not his own interests, but the other man's" (1 Corinthians 10:24, NEB). I'll buy that advice. It worked for me!

THE NEW YEAR'S EVE
I WON'T FORGET

BUDDY EBSEN

*Best known for his television roles in*The Beverly Hillbillies *and* Barnaby Jones,
Buddy Ebsen's movie career dates back to the 1930s.

The year 1945 was fading fast as my wife, Nancy, and I trudged home that evening in mid-Manhattan. Nancy had met me at a Broadway theater, where I had been rehearsing for my role in a revival of *Show Boat*. With heads lowered against the swirling snow, we headed back to our apartment.

Traffic sounds were muffled in that special hush that snow lends to harsh city streets. Nancy's boots crunched beside mine as we walked in silence, both lost in the kind of thoughts that the year's end brings.

It was a poignant time for us, as it was, I'm sure, for most people during the early post-World War II days when we all seemed to be finding our way again. In my case, I was trying to pick up the pieces of a career interrupted three years earlier when I had volunteered for Coast Guard service.

Serving aboard a ship in the forlorn reaches of the northern Pacific was a far cry from the singing and dancing I had been doing most of my life. And now, beginning all over again had me wondering what the future held. With war memories still churning within me, I felt unsettled, uneasy. Tap dancing on a stage didn't seem to make sense anymore.

I shook my head and squinted as wind whipped snow into my eyes. A clock in a jewelry store window indicated 11:30 P.M.

We had no plans for a New Year's Eve celebration; however, I did feel hungry. "Why don't we get a bite to eat before we go home?" I said, taking Nancy's arm.

My wife looked up over the muffler covering her face and nodded. A short distance ahead on 54th Street was a little place called Al & Dick's Steak House, where we had often dined. We quickened our steps, but when we reached the restaurant door, it was locked. Nancy and I glanced at each other in disappointment. But then, behind the curtained plate-glass window I could see shadows of people moving. I knocked on the door. It opened a bit and Al Green, one of the owners, peered out. A former pugilist with a broken nose, Al broke into a grin. "Hey, Buddy, Nancy, c'mon in," he said and he swung the door back.

It turned out that he and his partner, Dick, had invited all of their employees and spouses to a private New Year's Eve gathering. "Join us," urged Al, "you're part of the family."

And so we stepped into the warmth of the restaurant where couples laughed and chatted and loaded their plates with food from a mammoth buffet. Somewhere a piano tinkled. Nancy and I sat at a table and soon found ourselves caught up in the friendly atmosphere.

Suddenly, a hush fell over the restaurant.

I glanced at my watch; It was almost midnight. Soon the revelry would begin, I thought, expecting to see horns and noisemakers distributed. Instead, Al Green stepped to the center of the room and stood there as others settled at tables or against the wall.

"It's a tradition," whispered one of his waiters leaning over to us. "He does this every New Year's Eve."

As the big wall clock's hands lifted straight up, Al began to sing without accompaniment.

I was surprised by his rich, resonant voice; it didn't seem to go with his cauliflower ear and broken nose.

Our Father, which art in Heaven, he sang, *hallowed be Thy Name . . .*

I was transfixed. Al, who was Jewish, was singing to the Father of us all.

Thy kingdom come . . . he sang.

I was taken back to the little white-frame church in Belleville, Illinois, where I first learned this prayer.

Thy will be done on Earth, as it is in Heaven. Give us this day our daily bread and forgive us our debts, as we forgive our debtors. . . .

In a rush my thoughts turned back to my childhood days in Orlando, Florida; to the dancing school my father ran; to our minister telling me after a school play that I *must* go into show business; to my sister Vilma and me whirling to "Tea for Two," dancing our way across the country in shows and movies in those innocent-seeming years before the world was torn apart.

And lead us not into temptation; but deliver us from evil . . .

"Peace, dear Lord . . ." I silently prayed for the conciliation of all nations.

For Thine is the kingdom, and the power, and the glory, forever.

Al's voice rose powerfully and his words rang with conviction. And then, as the last firm note drifted away, Al lowered his head and he sang the last word as a benediction.

Amen.

Tears streamed down my face. Without taking my eyes off Al Green, I said to Nancy, "Never let me lose faith in God, in myself, or in people."

I could hear the noise outside of a city gone wild with celebration, but inside the restaurant there was a deep silence. It lasted only a moment, a moment in which I seemed to hear the noise and feel the confusion of the past three years. And then, as

I came back to the present, back to a restaurant on 54th Street in New York City, the war seemed to fade. I felt calm, reassured. I felt God's serenity.

When it was time for us to leave, Nancy and I put on our coats, and amid hearty good wishes from Al, Dick, and our "family," we walked out to the street. The snow had stopped. Everything was still, frosted with a neon iridescence. Tall buildings soared above us like church spires. The stars were like tiny sapphires winking in the deep blue.

"Happy New Year," I said to my wife.

"Yes, *Happy* New Year!" she said in reply as we stepped out confidently into a new year and a new world and a new beginning.

BE YOURSELF

CHARLES OSGOOD

*Charles Osgood has won two Emmy awards and a Peabody award
as host of CBS News'* Sunday Morning.

Maybe it looks easy—what I do on *CBS News Sunday Morning*. Maybe it sounds easy—what I do on "The Osgood File" weekday mornings on CBS Radio. People tell me it seems as if I were born to be on the air . . . little do they know.

It's true that our Creator endows us with the talent and temperament to do what he has in mind for us, but I'm afraid it was a challenge to get me to see that. I never took a broadcasting or journalism course in school. At Fordham University in New York, I majored in economics. In my spare time I worked at WFUV, the school's FM station in the Bronx. But that was an extracurricular activity that I thought might help me in establishing a career in the business side of broadcasting. Who knew that this would be my calling? Not me!

Even when the first job I landed after graduation was as an announcer at WGMS, a classical music station in Washington, D.C., it didn't register. Even when my assignment in the Army turned out to be working as the announcer for the U.S. Army Band's concerts, I had no idea it was leading me anywhere. I still thought management would be my career. And I seemed to be heading in that direction. After my stint in the Army, I became program director at WGMS. I was in management—finally.

Then came what I thought was my great opportunity. RKO General, the owner of WGMS, was starting the first experimental pay-television station in the United States, in Hartford, Connecticut, and I was named general manager. Unfortunately, subscription TV, as we called it, was an idea whose time had not yet come. I soon found out my time had not yet come either.

I had had visions of becoming a pay-television tycoon. One day, I thought, I would be to that medium what Bill Paley, the founder of CBS, had been to network radio and television. But apparently the Lord had other plans. I was fired. My boss came up from New York and gave me the bad news. I was crushed. I thought it was the worst thing that could ever happen to me.

While I looked for a new job, my wife and I moved in with my parents in New Jersey. I got rides into New York City with Dad's carpool. He was a textile executive; I was an unemployed pay-television tycoon. And because there weren't any pay-television stations except the one I'd been fired from, I wasn't even sure what kind of work I was looking for. A couple of months passed, and I began to wonder if I'd ever work again. This was not exactly a time of peak self-esteem for me. I'd see panhandlers on the street and identify strongly with them. I would think, there but for the grace of God go I.

One day I ran into an old friend from Fordham University on the street. Francis X. Maguire had worked with me at the college radio station. He had a job selling jingles. Frank had even tried to sell me a jingle when I was running the pay-television station in Hartford. Now he was working and I wasn't. So he gave me names of contacts and even went with me to see some New York broadcasting executives.

Believe it or not, a few weeks later, my old friend Frank became a New York broadcasting executive himself. ABC Radio hired him to co-produce a new show called "Flair Reports." For on-air talent, they were looking to hire five or six people to do news sidebars. Since they wanted the show to be new and different, they didn't want people with a lot of news experience. And I certainly qualified for that.

Frank urged me to come by the next week for an audition. "Write something and bring it in," he said.

"What should I write?" I asked. I'd never written more than a business letter.

"Write about whatever interests you," Frank told me. "Be yourself."

In the *New York Times,* I found what I thought was the perfect story. It was the obituary of a one-hundred-year-old former Metropolitan Opera diva. She had last sung half a century—half her lifetime—ago. I did my best to rough out some copy. At my audition, I read the story into the microphone, feeling as if my mouth were full of cotton. I could see the producers in the control room. Frank was the only one smiling. The others looked at me with *no* in their eyes. What did they care about a dead diva?

I left the studio dejected, knowing that I'd just had a terrible audition and blown a good opportunity. Frank caught up with me as I was walking down the hall. He looked me right in the eye and said, "You're hired. I know you can do this." His colleagues didn't want to hire me, but Frank had insisted. He knew what I could do, even if they didn't. Even if I didn't.

That same day he also hired a twenty-three-year-old desk assistant from a local radio station who hadn't been allowed on the air even once. Frank was a pretty good judge of talent, though. That kid was Ted Koppel. And that's how I, at age thirty, went from being one of the youngest television station general managers in the country to being its oldest cub radio reporter. I stayed at ABC doing "Flair Reports" and hourly newscasts for five years.

In 1967, I moved to CBS. I started at WCBS radio in New York, where I did newscasts in the middle of Pat Summerall's morning show. Then the station changed formats to all-news, and I became an anchor for the first time. Pat Summerall did the sports cut-ins. While still at WCBS, I began doing a radio network feature, "Newsbreak." One thing led to another, and I moved full-time to CBS News.

Those were the days of Cronkite, Collingwood, Sevareid, Moyers, and Kuralt. I was the only CBS newsman people had never heard of. My first newscast, filling in for Roger Mudd on a Saturday evening, was painful. I had never anchored television news before. I was so nervous and so bad that Mike Wallace called me into his office and gave me some pointers. They were helpful too.

All of this led in due course to *The Osgood File* and, when Charles Kuralt retired, to *CBS News Sunday Morning*, a broadcast that seeks to show the positive, noble side of human nature. While not every single one of our stories has a happy ending, we try to make each one uplifting.

I consider myself the luckiest man in broadcasting. But believe me, it didn't come easily. Maybe I was meant to do this, but I had to be dragged into it kicking and screaming. It's a good thing the Lord stuck with me, or I might never have found the work I love. And finding that, I have to say, is one of the happiest endings I know.

The
Importance
of
Persistence

THE TALENT I DIDN'T KNOW I HAD

MICHAEL LANDON

Michael Landon starred in a number of television series, including
Bonanza, Little House on the Prairie, *and* Highway to Heaven.

*I*f there's one thing I can't stand people saying, it's "I'm no good at anything . . . I don't have any talent." I just don't buy that at all. To me, everyone has at least one talent, and while it sometimes takes you a lifetime to find, it *does* exist.

There was a time, of course, when I didn't believe that. What changed my mind was a seemingly small event that took place back in 1953.

At that time I was a skinny little high school sophomore in Collingswood, New Jersey, a town just across the Delaware River from Philadelphia. At Collingswood High I was a good student, but as far as I was concerned, in just about every other department I was a loser. As a funny-looking pip-squeak named Eugene Orowitz, who weighed barely a hundred pounds, I desperately wanted to fit in, to be something and do something well. But because I hadn't found anything I was good at, I looked upon myself as being a total flop.

One sunny afternoon during the spring of that year, our gym class went out to the school's running track. The teacher was going to acquaint us all with various track and field events. We were shown hurdles, the broad jump, the pole vault. I stumbled weakly through them all.

"Now we'll try the javelin," the teacher said.

I watched as he picked up a gleaming metal spear about six feet long and gave it a short toss. Suddenly I was captivated and didn't know why. Something inside me began saying, "Try it! Try it!"

I had to wait my turn, though, because several others wanted a crack at the javelin too. Shy and scared, I watched them, trying not to look too eager. Finally, when everyone had had a chance to throw—the longest heave going about thirty yards—I looked at the teacher.

"Hey, Orowitz, you want to try?" he asked.

Embarrassed, I looked down, but managed to nod my head.

"Well, come on then," he said impatiently, and handed me the javelin. Behind me I could hear some of my classmates chuckling.

"Think you can lift it, Ugy?" one said.

"Don't stab yourself," another added, laughing.

As I grasped the javelin in my hand, I was seized with a strange feeling—a new-found excitement. Seeing myself as a Roman warrior about to do battle, my fears vanished. For some crazy reason, I was relaxed over what I was about to do, even though I'd never done it before.

I raised the javelin over my head, took six quick steps, and then let the thing go. The same voice that had urged me into throwing it, now told me it was a good throw. I watched as the spear took off. While other students' throws had wobbled or turned cockeyed in the air, to my surprise, my throw was traveling straight and true.

My heart quickened as I saw it continue to sail, thirty yards out, then forty. As it went past the fifty-yard mark, it was still going when it went crashing down beyond some empty bleachers.

For a minute nothing was said. Then someone whispered, "Holy cow!" and others began cheering and slapping me on the back. Nobody could believe what little

Orowitz had just done. Neither could I, really. And when I think back on it, the whole scene must have resembled something out of a B movie.

I ran to retrieve the javelin and when I found it, I saw the tip had been broken off in landing. Expecting a real bawling out, I took the javelin back to the gym teacher.

"Don't worry about it," he said, still shaking his head in wonder. "You keep it."

That night I took the javelin home with me and, much to my parents' astonishment, never let it out of my sight. The very next day I began practicing with it, and every day that summer—for six hours or more—I would throw it in a nearby schoolyard. The joy of finding something I could do made me determined to do as well in it as I could.

By the time I was a senior and a member of the track team, all my practice paid off. I threw the javelin 211 feet that year, the best throw by any high school boy in the country.

That record gave me a track scholarship to the University of Southern California. With my eye on the Olympics, I continued to work out until one day in college, after not warming up properly, I tore some ligaments in my left shoulder. While I still could throw, I was never able to achieve the distance I once could, so I gave up my track scholarship and my dream of the Olympics.

Though that was a terrible disappointment, I've learned since then that as we are developing one talent, others seem to spring from it without our realizing it. While the javelin gave me a chance to go to college, it also provided me with a new-found confidence and the ability to shed my inferiority complex. I was able to see the importance of that when, after I dropped out of USC, I took a job in a Los Angeles warehouse. There, a co-worker, an aspiring actor, asked my help in learning his part in a small playhouse production of *Home of the Brave*.

When I began reading the script, I became mesmerized. The same kind of fascination that took hold of me when I picked up the javelin now led me to drama. Immediately I enrolled in acting school. That led to small parts in movies, which in turn brought me the role of Little Joe Cartwright in *Bonanza*. That TV series lasted fourteen years and it led me to still another area—directing *Little House on the Prairie*.

I'm convinced that everyone has some kind of hidden talent. God sees to it—it's that simple. The difficult part for some of us is in finding the talent. That's why I feel strongly that we must keep our minds open; we can't let ourselves be discouraged or depressed when the talent doesn't readily appear. Yet when it does, we must be prepared to grab hold of it right away.

Whenever I think about what made that scrawny kid pick up that javelin, I know there was a reason. God was on that high school field whispering to me, "Here's an opportunity. Take it." And am I glad I listened to Him—glad I trusted my enthusiasm—for I not only found my talent, but I truly found myself.

SOMEONE IS WATCHING

COLIN L. POWELL

*Colin Powell served as chairman of the Joint Chiefs of Staff for
President George H. W. Bush; he was nominated and confirmed as
Secretary of State for President George W. Bush in 2001.*

In 1991 I faced an enjoyable yet formidable challenge. I was
returning to my old neighborhood in the South Bronx to speak to
the students of my old school, Morris High. As we drove down streets
where my friend Gene Norman and I used to race bicycles, I thought of the pitfalls
awaiting the kids living there: the drugs, the temptations, the crime. What could I
say to encourage them?

As we passed the hamburger place that I used to haunt, I remembered my
growing-up years here, the joys, the sorrows, the choices. Even then kids faced
choices. There were drugs in my neighborhood and a youngster could gain easy
access to them if tempted. But in my family, the decision was simple: you just
didn't do it. We knew it was stupid and the most self-destructive thing you could
do with the life God had given you.

Dad and Mom had moved to America from Jamaica. They both worked hard in
the garment district, Dad as a shipping clerk, Mom as a seamstress. Our folks gave
my sister and me structure and direction; they made it clear they had high expectations for us. And kids usually live up to expectations.

Moreover, their guidance was buttressed by an extended family of aunts, uncles,
and cousins all living in the area, keeping an eye on us. Someone was always watch-

ing. But that "someone" would be far more than just family, I was to learn.

At age seventeen I found a summer job in a local soft drink bottling plant at ninety cents an hour. I was thrilled. On my first day of work, having joined the ranks of other newly hired teenagers, I was full of enthusiasm. The bottling machines caught my eye, but only the white boys worked there. I was hired as a porter and my foreman handed me a mop.

I got to work. I mopped what seemed like acres of sticky, cola-stained floor. Today as I talk to young people who may face the same frustrations, I tell a story that mirrors my experience.

It seems there were three men who were ditch diggers. They'd be out there every day, except that one guy would be leaning on his shovel talking about how one day he was going to own the company. The second guy leaned on his shovel and complained they didn't pay him enough. But the third guy just kept on digging.

Years went by, and the first guy was still leaning on that shovel telling how one of these days he was going to own the company. The second guy was still complaining about the hours and pay. But the third guy was now driving a forklift truck.

More years passed; the first guy, now gray-headed, still leaned on that shovel, saying, "One of these days I'm going to own this company." The second guy had retired on disability after a phony injury. And the third guy? He owned the company.

For me, that story has a moral to it. It says that in whatever you do, someone is always watching. Perhaps I was conscious of that fact as a teenager, for I decided to be the best mop wielder there ever was. Right to left, left to right. One day someone let fifty cases of cola crash to the cement, and brown, sticky foam cascaded across the floor. It was almost more than I could bear. But I kept on mopping. Right to left, left to right.

At summer's end the foreman said, "You mop floors pretty good."

"You sure gave me enough opportunity to learn, sir," I said.

The next summer he put me to work loading bottles on the filling machine. The third summer I was deputy foreman.

Someone far more important was also watching, I learned. We Powells faithfully attended St. Margaret's Episcopal Church in the Bronx, where Dad was senior warden. I'll never forget when I was confirmed, the bishop laying his hands on my head and intoning, "Defend, O Lord, this thy child with thy heavenly grace; that he may continue thine forever; and daily increase in thy Holy Spirit more and more, until he comes unto thy everlasting kingdom. Amen."

Those words gave me a deep assurance, and every year thereafter when I heard this supplication, that feeling of God watching over me was reaffirmed. Along with it was a sense of needing to live up to his expectations, and my family made it clear this involved getting all the education we could. Dad had never finished high school. "I want you to do better than I have," he emphasized.

Though I was in the "slow" class as a fourth-grader at P.S. 39 and a C student in high school, I managed to squeeze into City College of New York. Its main attraction was the tuition, ten dollars a year. My grades weren't the best, but I did well in the Reserve Officers' Training Corps. In fact, had it not been for ROTC, I might not have had the grades to graduate. The Army felt right to me, and when I graduated I was commissioned as a second lieutenant. Some folks in my family wondered: "Cousin Johnny went into law, cousin Cecilia is studying medicine, and here Colin, of all things, is going into the Army. He isn't in trouble or anything?" But Dad and Mom gave me their blessing.

Within four years of my 1958 graduation from college, I was assigned to Vietnam, where I began to find the truth in the adage that even when necessary, war is a terrible thing.

In 1963 I went to Fort Benning, Georgia, followed by further studies at the Army Command and General Staff College located at Fort Leavenworth, Kansas. There I became interested in opportunities for an advanced degree in graduate school. This became a shining goal, and I decided I would apply despite only average college grades.

I'd come to recognize the value of striving to learn as much in and about life as I could. In fact, by that time I clearly recognized that one had to work especially hard for the things that were of value and importance. Out of a graduating class of 1,244 at Command and General State College, I ranked second. Upon graduation in 1968, I was sent back to Vietnam.

Not long afterward, the *Army Times* ran an article about the staff college's top five students. Again someone was watching. When my division commander in Vietnam saw the story, he pulled me in from the field to be his operations chief.

In 1969 my opportunity for graduate school finally came. I entered George Washington University, where I earned a master's degree in business administration.

In the twenty years that followed, I held many military commands and served in the Pentagon and at the White House. In 1989 President George H. W. Bush appointed me chairman of the Joint Chiefs of Staff. I held that position when I returned to the Bronx.

My old school hadn't changed much. As I walked up its familiar stone steps, I remembered racing up them to beat the bell. The setting for my talk to the student body was the gymnasium.

"I remember this place," I told the students. "I remember it all. I remember running through Van Cortlandt Park with the track team, the route I used to take each day from my home on Kelly Street to school.

"I also remember, upon occasion, experiencing the feeling 'You can't make it,' " I continued. "But you can. When I was growing up, opportunities were limited. But now the opportunities are there to be anything you want to be. But wanting to be isn't enough, dreaming about it isn't enough. You've got to study for it, work for it, fight for it with all your heart, energy and soul, so that nothing will be denied you."

I wanted them to make the right choices, to work hard, and to not lose sight of a dream. And I wanted them to know that someone is always watching.

NEIL ARMSTRONG'S BOYHOOD CRISIS

MRS. STEPHEN ARMSTRONG
AS TOLD TO LORRAINE WETZEL

Neil Armstrong will always be remembered for his historic words:
"That's one small step for a man; one giant leap for mankind."

ost people think Neil Armstrong took the most important step in his life when he set foot on the moon. But as his mother, I remember an even greater step taken in our old home on Pearl Street in Wapakoneta, Ohio, on another July day—twenty-three years earlier.

The story begins when Neil was just two years old, and his father and I lived in Cleveland, not far from the airport. Like many families during the Depression days of the early 1930s, one of our inexpensive Sunday afternoon pastimes was airplane watching. Neil would stand between us, with his little face pressed so intently against the fence that it often left red marks. We were always ready to leave long before Neil was, and his plea was always the same: "Can't we see just one more airplane?"

I was often uneasy about Neil's obvious fascination with planes. And I had to admit to myself that this child, our firstborn, was very special to me. After Stephen and I married, I was haunted by the fear that maybe I couldn't conceive. I had been an only child and often thought, what if I can't have even one baby?

Then finally the day came when our doctor assured me I was pregnant. The minute I got home I went down on my knees and thanked God for his blessing, and, in the fullness of my heart, I dedicated this child-to-be to him. In the months that followed, I prayed steadily that this child would be given a thirst for knowledge and the capacity for learning that someday would accomplish noble deeds—hopefully to serve the work of the Lord.

One Sunday morning, when Neil was five or six, he and my husband left for Sunday school. When they returned, both had peculiar expressions on their faces. Stephen was a bit white-faced, but Neil was beaming from ear to ear.

"What is wrong with you two?" I asked. There was utter silence.

Suddenly a thought came to me. "Did you go up in that airplane I read about in the paper?"

Now they looked relieved. Yes, that was exactly what they had done. A pilot was barnstorming in town, and Stephen said rates were cheaper in the morning. He had not really enjoyed the flight, but little Neil had loved every minute of it.

One morning Neil and I walked down the cluttered aisles of a dime store looking for cereal bowls. My husband and I now had a wonderful family of three active children who consumed vast quantities of cereal. Somehow the bowls were always getting chipped or broken. I was selecting five shiny new ones when I felt a tug at my arm. "Mom, will you buy this for me?" Neil said as he held up a gaily colored box.

"What is it?" I asked cautiously.

"It's a model-airplane kit." The eagerness in his voice betrayed his excitement. "Mom, this way I can learn how to make airplanes. It's twenty cents."

Quickly I thought about how twenty cents would buy two cereal bowls, but how could I resist the urgency and enthusiasm in my son's voice?

"Honey," I said gently, "can you find a kit for ten cents?"

"Sure, Mom!" His face radiant, he raced back to the toy counter.

Although Neil was then only eight years old, that was the beginning of two important occupations in his life. The first was his meticulous assembly line for many model airplanes. We put a table in one corner of the living room, and it was never moved—even when company came.

The second occupation made the first one possible. Beginning with his first model plane, Neil was never without a job, no matter how small. First he cut grass in a cemetery for ten cents an hour. Later he cleaned out the bread mixer at Neumeister's Bakery every night. After we moved to Wapakoneta, Neil delivered orders for the neighborhood grocery, swept out the hardware store, and opened cartons at Rhine and Brading's Pharmacy.

When Neil wasn't working or studying, he rode his bicycle three miles north on a gravel road to the Wapak Flying Service Airport. Today this field isn't used, but in 1944 it bustled with activity. A young instructor, Charles Finkenbine, kept three light airplanes busy as trainers. Budding pilots came from surrounding counties to learn to fly; and Neil at fourteen was a familiar figure sitting on the sidelines, his eyes glued to every takeoff and landing. One afternoon I was making grape jelly when the screen door banged as he rushed into the kitchen.

"Mom," he shouted, "Mr. Finkenbine let me *touch* one of the airplanes!"

"That's fine, son," I said.

"He says from now on I can be a grease monkey and one of these days he'll teach me to fly!"

"Are you sure you're old enough, Neil?" I tried to hide the anxiety in my voice.

He flashed his wide, confident grin. "Don't worry. I'll be careful."

The screen door banged again, and he was gone. I'm afraid his assurance did little to comfort me. By now I was beginning to wonder how the Lord could be served by a youngster so completely captivated by airplanes.

From then on, every penny Neil earned went for flying lessons. At forty cents an hour at the pharmacy, it took him between twenty-two and twenty-three hours of work to pay for one nine-dollar lesson. But both Dick Brading and Charles Finkenbine were generous men: The first often let Neil off early to go to the airport. The latter arranged free flying time for our son in exchange for odd jobs around the hangar. Neil's goal was to get his flying license as soon as he reached his sixteenth birthday in August.

In July our two boys, Neil and Dean, with their father as scoutmaster, attended Boy Scout camp in Defiance, Ohio. The evening they were due back I planned a special homecoming supper. They thought they'd be home at five o'clock, so I peeled potatoes and put them on to boil at 4:30, then started to set the table.

At 5:15 I picked up my darning basket and started to mend some of Dean's socks. An hour dragged by. I finished the socks and walked to the window. They were more than an hour overdue, and I knew something was wrong.

Then, looking through the grape arbor, I saw our car drive into the garage. My husband appeared in the doorway, his face pale and drawn. Fear clutched my throat.

"What's wrong, Stephen? Has something happened to the boys?"

"No, they're all right. Dean is here with me, and Neil will be along soon. But there has been an accident."

"What do you mean?"

"Viola, come into the living room, and I'll tell you all about it." He put his arm around me, and together we walked to the sofa.

"We were on our way home this afternoon," he continued, "when we noticed an airplane flying parallel to us. Neil recognized it immediately as one of the trainers from the Wapak Flying Service. Some student was practicing takeoffs and landings in a field near the road. Then he must have dipped too low over the telephone wires, because suddenly the airplane was in trouble."

"Oh, no!" I whispered.

"It nosedived into the field, and at the same time Neil yelled, 'Stop the car!' Before I knew it, he had climbed over the fence and was running toward the plane. Then we all got out and ran over to help too. Neil was lifting a young fellow out of the cockpit, and just as we got there he died in Neil's arms."

"Oh, Stephen, how awful! That poor boy and his family." Then a terrifying new thought seared my brain. "It might have been Neil."

"Yes, Viola, it could have been." My husband's voice roughened with emotion. "Instead it was a young man from Lima whom Neil knew. Neil is staying with him until the ambulance comes."

A car door slammed, and I heard slow footsteps coming up the porch steps. Suddenly Neil and I were in each other's arms, tears streaming down our faces.

"He was my friend, Mom. And he was *only* twenty!" I could hardly bear the anguish in his voice.

"I know, honey." I released him, with a mother's sudden awareness that her son was no longer a boy. I forced my voice to sound cheerful. "Do you want some supper?"

"No, thanks, I'm going up to my room." He stopped on the landing and tried to smile. "Don't worry, Mom. I'll be all right."

"I know you will, Neil." I watched him walk up the stairs and quietly close the door as dry sobs tore through me.

Stephen and I both thought it best to leave him alone for a while. But we could not help wondering if Neil would want to keep flying. Both of us agreed he must fight this battle himself.

The next two days were the hardest of my life. As all mothers know, whatever hurts your children hurts you twice as much. And yet I knew he had to make this decision himself. Had our closeness with the Creator and the nightly prayers through the years prepared him to find the help he needed so desperately now? At this stage, it was out of my hands. All I could do was wait.

I tried to carry on a normal family life, but my heart and mind were always in that back bedroom with the iron bed, yellow wallpaper, the single overhead light fixture, and the bureau covered with model airplanes. What was he thinking? What would he decide?

Finally, near dusk on the second day, I couldn't stand the silence and separation any longer. I baked oatmeal and raisin cookies and took a plate of them and a glass of cold milk upstairs.

"Neil, may I come in, please? Here are some cookies still warm from the oven."

He opened the door, and I walked into the stuffy little room and put the cookies on the bureau. What I saw made my heart leap. Next to a model airplane was an old Sunday-school notebook with a picture of Jesus on the cover. It was now turned to the page where years before Neil had written in his large childish hand, "The Character of Jesus," and had listed ten qualities of his. Among those that caught my eye were: He was sinless. He was humble. He championed the poor. He was unselfish. But the one that struck me most was number eight—he was close to God.

Suddenly I felt like singing hosanna. "Honey, what have you decided about flying?" I asked him.

Neil's eyes held mine in a steady gaze, then he said firmly, "Mom, I hope you and Dad will understand, but with God's help, I *must* go on flying."

For a minute I was jolted as I thought of that other mother only a few miles away in Lima, brokenhearted and perhaps standing in her son's empty room at this very minute. I asked God for strength and the right words, and he gave them to me.

"All right, son. Dad and I will go along with your decision." My heart was pounding. "And, Neil," I said, "when you get your license in a few weeks, may I be your first passenger?"

THE WAYWARD ARROW

BEAU BRIDGES

Beau Bridges first appeared on screen at the age of seven. He won an Emmy for his portrayal of former press secretary James Brady in Without Warning.

*W*hen was the first time you became aware of God? For me, it happened in an odd way when I was a kid. It was the summer when archery was the craze among my friends. And, of all things, it was an arrow that first led me to think about God.

I was a boy, just twelve, growing up in Mar Vista, California. My father, Lloyd Bridges, was a film actor, and my brother Jeff, my sister Lucinda, and I did the same kinds of things other kids did—like mowing lawns for extra money and playing softball. We had chores around the house, and we loved hanging out with friends.

In fact, I was hanging out with a bunch of my pals the day this strange thing happened. We had brought our bows and arrows to a field about two miles from my house. We had made our own arrows that summer, gluing colored feathers to the ends and painting the shafts so that each was unique. That day I was using my favorite arrow; it had red dots outlined in black, and I'd stuck black and red feathers on the end. There was no classier and, I felt, no swifter arrow in my collection.

We weren't using targets. Instead we were playing a game we'd created on our own—one of those crazy, "death-defying" games that boys that age seem to love. We'd played this game many times that summer, and the fact that it was dangerous only heightened the excitement.

We would stand in a tightly knit group in the middle of the field. Each of us would put an arrow on his bowstring, then pull it back and raise the bow so that the arrow was pointing up, perpendicular to the ground. Then someone would call out, "Let 'em fly," and we would all shoot our arrows at once.

The arrows would zoom up into the sky, out of sight. Then we'd listen for their return. We knew that, having flown straight up, they would be falling straight down, and we huddled in morbid anticipation, hoping they wouldn't be hitting *us*. The object of the game, you see, was to have the arrows land as close to the group as possible, without, of course, hurting anyone. The winner was the owner of the arrow that hit the nearest.

That day when I heard the call, "Let 'em fly," my bowstring reverberated with a loud zing and I watched the polka-dotted shaft of my favorite arrow whiz up into the sun's rays and disappear. Soon we heard *zump . . . zump, zump*, and the arrows began falling all around us. When they stopped, everyone rushed to claim his, and several of the fellows shouted. "Mine is the closest!" I looked around, but *mine* was missing. It was strange. My arrow should have landed close to the others, but there was no trace of it.

I covered every inch of the field, and my friend Chuck Bylor helped, but we couldn't find it. Doggedly, I continued searching. I was disappointed, and felt a little silly . . . and puzzled. Where was it? Mine went up with the rest. It should have come down with the rest. It made me feel, well, kind of eerie.

Earlier I had promised to help Chuck mow a neighbor's lawn. Chuck was ready to go to our job, but I wanted to search some more.

"Come on," he yelled at me, "it's time to go."

"Let's look just a few more minutes," I begged. "It's *bound* to be here."

"Look," said Chuck, "you promised to help me this afternoon. Now, c'mon, we've *got* to go!"

It's funny how something as small as an arrow can mean so much to you when you're twelve. But I felt strangely sad, as though I'd lost a kind of friend. A lot of myself had gone into making it. I had shown it to my father and friends, and everyone had complimented me and made a big deal over it.

And now it was gone. Probably buried in the matted grass. I visualized it snapping under the weight of someone's foot, and groaned. And now I had to go help Chuck; I couldn't back out of that. I had promised.

Have you ever wished very hard for something, with all your energy, even though you knew it would be incredible if it ever really happened? Well, that's how it was with me and that arrow. While I was helping Chuck cut grass, I daydreamed about finding it.

When we finished our work, I waved "so long" to Chuck and headed home. Then, for some reason I can't explain, I was suddenly bursting with energy. I felt good! I wanted to run. And did I ever! I raced at top speed down the street. I charged along not knowing the reason for my elation, and then, out of breath, I slowed down to a walk. Ahead of me was a great tree whose branches reached out across the pathway. My clothes were sticking to my sweaty body, and my breath was coming in great gasps; the tree offered welcome shade from the sun, and as I drew nearer, I lifted my head up slightly and felt grateful for the coolness.

My eyes rested for a moment on the tree's gnarled branches; the leaves fluttered. Something red and black fluttered too. I glanced down along the trunk and over to the other side of the tree, but the bit of red and black pulled my eyes back. A bird? . . . No . . . My brain did a double take, and I came to a startled halt. I blinked. Yes! There it was! My arrow! Two miles from where I had shot it!

I felt happy and bewildered all at once. The question—how did it get there?—kept turning in my mind. Could it have been carried along on a wind current, then dropped down into the tree? That seemed unlikely. And why *this* tree, along *this* path? Could some kids have found it and thrown it up into the branches? Still, no one—not even I—knew I'd be coming down this path; there were other ways home. Why did I choose this one? How did I happen to look up just in time to see the black and red feathers?

I was stumped. The arrow couldn't have traveled two miles on the power I had used in drawing back on the bowstring when I let it fly. I knew I wasn't that strong.

"Gee," I said out loud. I reached up to grab the arrow. Something superhuman, superstrong, something so immense that I couldn't understand it was involved here. It made me feel a little weird, a little scared. As I took my arrow in hand again, a shiver ran down my spine.

That was the moment when I had my very first intimation of God.

It was a little thing, my finding that arrow, but it was something that had happened to *me*—it was my own special mystery. For the first time in my life I had to accept something I couldn't understand, and I was in awe of it.

From that day on I began attending church and Sunday school with new interest, learning about faith, talking to God, praying the Lord's Prayer—which became a part of my daily life. As I grew older, I discovered that my experience with the arrow that summer's day was but a tiny sample of what religion is all about. Faith in God is a mixture of mystery and awe; you cannot see it or touch it; it requires only that we accept and believe.

And that has been my understanding of faith ever since. It is something that I like to talk about to my own sons. Yet I wonder if they can really comprehend my story. I wonder if faith doesn't come to everyone differently, in some mysterious way.

MY ROUGH ROAD TO OBEDIENCE

ROGER STAUBACH

As quarterback for the Dallas Cowboys, Roger Staubach led the team to four NFC titles and two Super Bowl championships.

ife took on extra excitement the day they began to build the new house next door to us. I was about seven, an only child, with a yearning for adventure. Aware of my fascination with the construction next door, Dad warned me, "You are not to go near that new house."

"Why?"

"Because you might get hurt."

Rebellious, I watched the house develop, floor by floor. The painters came and the house took on real luster. After the workers had mixed cement and carefully spread it on the front walk, the temptation to get a close look was too much. How could I get hurt when the house was almost finished?

Late in the afternoon, after the workers had all gone home and while Mother seemed to be quite involved in the basement, I crept stealthily into the forbidden territory and sat down beside the new cement walk. Carefully, I placed the palm of my right hand facedown on the wet cement. It felt soft and cool. For a moment I studied the imprint of my hand on the walk. Then I placed my left hand on the cement.

"Hey, kid. Get outa there!"

Alarmed, I looked up. Striding toward me was a man whom I recognized as the supervisor. Like a startled fawn I bolted back into my house, the man in hot pursuit. From under the bed of my room I heard the doorbell ring, then voices in the living room.

That night I got it. First, a spanking from my father. Then came the worst part—I was forbidden to use the playground across the street for two weeks.

Along with the punishment came an explanation that no family could function properly unless children obeyed their parents, and that my disobedience had resulted in damage to property.

There were other times when I was disobedient and needed correction; but my parents, while firm, were always fair and loving about it. And it didn't take many punishments for me to see something very clearly: When I messed up, there was unhappiness in our home and I was miserable. When I obeyed the rules set down by my parents, there was harmony and contentment in our family.

Since my father made a rather unpredictable income as representative for a shoe firm, economy and discipline were essential in our home. Mother took a job when I was nine, so this meant shared duties all around.

And yet, while our rules were important, the more I accepted responsibility, the more freedom and flexibility there were for me as I went from junior high on through high school.

Perhaps this is why the strict rules at the Naval Academy were so hard to take when I entered there in 1959. I could accept the need for order and routine, and even the ribbing that plebes had to take from upperclassmen. But the time spent on keeping my shoes looking like mirrors and memorizing a lot of wordy regulations seemed so pointless.

My rebellion flared. Soon demerits were being posted in my record book, like points on the scoreboard during a high scoring basketball game. I collected over one hundred demerits the first six months.

I was having academic problems as well, in metallurgy and mechanical drawing. It began to look as if my stay at Annapolis would be a very short one.

I suppose it was a combination of factors that helped straighten me out: good advice from my parents, plus the counsel of a young instructor who had graduated from the academy only a few years before.

"Roger, I know some of these rules seem like nonsense to you," he told me. "You and others think we're behind the times here at the academy. Changes will come—slowly. But the main purpose behind these regulations is to teach obedience. If military men don't learn to obey an order—whether they like it or not—we'll have chaos in our armed forces. In addition to that, I'm convinced that obedience is the key to the contented life."

When I did shape up, it worked out just as the instructor said. My grades went up, the demerits stopped accumulating, and one day I suddenly realized that I loved the place.

What then followed was a great football experience at Navy, but much more important than the awards and honors from football was learning something about that very elusive quality of leadership. To become a leader, I learned that you first have to be willing to accept authority.

But when I finished my stint in the Navy and joined the Dallas Cowboys in 1968, I found that once again, I still had something to learn about obedience. For what I loved so much about being quarterback for the Navy football team back in 1961–1963 was the feeling that I was in command of an eleven-man unit.

The quarterback of a football team directs the attack. He usually calls the plays in a huddle after getting advice and information from his teammates. The coach will occasionally send in instructions from the sidelines, but the quarterback is considered the commander of the offensive field unit.

But it didn't work out that way a few years later when Dallas won the professional football championship. At the beginning of the season, two quarterbacks were competing for the number one position on the Dallas team—Craig Morton and I. Our coach, Tom Landry, alternated us for the first seven games.

One day he told me, "Roger, from now on you're my number one quarterback."

I was elated, of course, but soon found myself chafing at the conditions. As a quarterback of a team of outstanding players, I was only a partial leader. Coach Tom Landry called the plays, sending in his instructions during our huddles. I threw passes only when he said to, used the running plays he called. In an emergency situation, I could change a play on the line of scrimmage if I felt it was right—but I had better be right!

I'll admit it—a lot of the problem was ego, my ego. With Coach Landry calling the plays, the implication was, of course, that quarterback Staubach was not good enough to know what plays to call.

When I was willing to go through a spiritual struggle to get self out of the way, the real facts emerged. I was darn lucky to be the number one quarterback of one of the best teams in pro football. I was inexperienced and had a lot to learn about play calling in the pros. Coach Landry had a rare "genius minds" when it came to football strategy. We were winning, and I was playing well with our coach sending in the plays.

So again I faced up to the issue of obedience, suddenly aware of how it confronts you in different ways at different times in your life. What happened then was the same thing that happened in my home and at the Naval Academy. Once I learned to obey, I found harmony, fulfillment, and victory.

The point still had to be rammed home in one more area of my life. This occurred at the birth of our fourth child. We were all greatly anticipating this big event—my wife, Marianne, and our three young daughters, Jennifer, Michele, and Stephanie Marie.

But during the delivery something went wrong. The baby girl was stillborn.

I'll never forget that day at the cemetery, when the tiny casket was lowered into the ground over which was the simple inscription "Baby Staubach." This was a very trying period in my life, for my father had passed away a year earlier.

As so many do in such personal crises, I asked the question, "Why, Lord?" Inside me once again were the stirrings of rebellion, this time against the Almighty who had such power over life and death.

It wasn't a long rebellion. Deep down I knew that strength came through my faith. When I prayed for understanding, I felt this sudden sense of peace and comfort. The Lord was Lord. He was with my daughter and my father. This world is not the end, but the beginning. If we believe in him, there is the promise of eternal life.

Out of this acceptance has come gratitude for all he has given me: a strong body, a clear mind, fine parents, a wife and three daughters whom I love very much, and a career doing what I like most to do—play football. The old prophet Isaiah was right on target when he said, "If ye be willing and obedient, ye shall eat the good of the land"(Isaiah 1:19, KJV).

Strength Through Scripture

SMALL GRACES

TERRY ANDERSON

Former journalist Terry Anderson was held hostage in Beirut for 2,455 days, longer than any of the other American hostages captured at that time.

A t the time it was a mystery. Why was I led to that old church? It had happened in the fall of 1984 when my fiancée, Madeleine, and I were visiting her family in Sunderland, a town in northern England. I had looked forward to peace and quiet, a respite from my hectic career. After six years as a Marine Corps correspondent for Armed Forces Television and Radio Service in Vietnam, I had joined the Associated Press, reporting disasters, plane hijacks, rebellions, and, for the past several years, covering the ongoing violence in Lebanon.

I was so dispirited that it took me some days to settle down, even in the pleasant atmosphere of this English hamlet. As we strolled its neat streets, inhaling the crisp, early winter air, I noticed a church steeple outlined against the pale blue sky. Although I had been brought up in the Catholic church back in Batavia, New York, I had drifted far from God and considered myself an agnostic. Why did that tall gray spire keep catching my eye?

After a few days in Sunderland, I finally decided to walk over to the church. When I got there I pulled open the heavy oaken door, stepped in and settled into a worn pew. Looking up at the altar and at the cross gleaming in the shadows, I suddenly had a strong sense of coming home. This was where I belonged. I believed in God the Father, his Son, Christ Jesus, and his Holy Spirit.

For the next six months back at work I tried to sort through this revelation. What did it mean in my life? What was I required to do? I was beginning to sense a closer relationship with God when, one morning on a street in Beirut, I was shoved at gunpoint into the back of a green Mercedes. My face was pressed to the floor and a blanket thrown over me as the car accelerated. It was March 16, 1985.

I lay on a cot for twenty-four days, eyes covered by a blindfold, chains painfully tight on my wrists and ankles. Finally, as shoes scraped the floor nearby, I gasped in Arabic, "Hey, *chebab*" (mister).

The footsteps halted.

"You can't do this to me," I said. "I'm a man, not an animal. I'll go crazy."

"What do you want?"

"A Bible."

He left without another word. The next day something thudded on my cot. My chains were loosened; I sat up. The blindfold was removed, but the blanket was pulled over my head so that I couldn't see anything except the book on my lap.

It was a Bible, the Revised Standard Version, red cover.

In the past I had read parts of the Bible on an intellectual level. Now I scoured its pages, book by book. I read it through, ten times, twenty, fifty. Each time, I found something new to sustain me. A verse that inspired me one week filled me with even greater illumination the next. Why haven't I seen that before? I wondered.

I read the Old Testament along with the new, flashing back and forth, finding fascinating correlations and insights. And after a while, a marvelous thing happened. The Bible characters came to life! I knew them as living beings: the hopeful, poetic Isaiah; the stentorian Jeremiah; the holy, pure, young Mary of Nazareth.

Amid the filth, the beatings, and the chains that shackled me to a wall, I felt so close to the long-suffering Job. I cried out to God with him, "I'm a good man. Why are you doing this to me? It's not fair!"

God answered, *It doesn't have to be fair. I'm going to do what I want and you have to accept it.*

So it was that I began to learn acceptance.

Can anyone speak better to a man in chains than Paul, who wrote so often from a prison cell? I sensed the hidden worth in his suffering: "I want you to know, brethren, that what has happened to me has really served to advance the gospel" (Philippians 1:12, RSV).

I found Paul both fascinating and frustrating. He has such a beauty, a sense of Christ's presence, and then he says something that irritates me, revealing him as a difficult and tortured man. In this I found solace too, knowing this saint.

One of my worst ordeals was looking back on my thirty-seven years to see things I was ashamed of. Peter helped me here. I had come to know him as the stumbling saint. He kept getting it wrong, and Jesus kept patting him on the back, saying, "It's okay. Don't worry about it." Like Peter, I could reconcile myself to the fact that I had done some bad things and would probably do more in the future. But that need not prevent me from finding forgiveness in Christ. God doesn't ask us to be perfect, I felt, but to try to live better than we do.

Months and then years ground on, each dismal day a dull blur of boredom, punctuated by cruelty, bad food and sickness. Most torturous of all was the deep aching I felt for my family and loved ones.

My captors moved me from one secret location to another, wrapped like a mummy head to toe in plastic tape, with only my nostrils exposed. I was transported in a car trunk or, worse, in a hidden compartment under a truck. As we bumped along potholed pavements, exhaust fumes filled the narrow compartment, burning my nostrils; I was overcome with nausea, and struggled to keep from throwing up, knowing I would strangle on my vomit. I calmed myself with the rosary's hypnotic repetition: "Hail Mary, full of grace . . ."

When I learned of my father's death, and then my brother's, I could only pray with David: "Why hast thou forsaken me? Why art thou so far from helping me, from the words of my groaning?" (Psalm 22:1, RSV).

Then God sent me a mouse. It arrived one day when some of us captives were kept in a dank, dark subbasement. I learned that if I placed a piece of bread on my shoulder and kept still, he would come up and nibble it. The mouse became a friend, showing up quite regularly. Eventually he disappeared, but not before my spirits were lifted.

Again and again amid our grinding ordeal, small graces came, which helped us survive. Among the hostages was Father Martin Jenko. We conducted worship services twice a day in what we wryly called the Church of the Locked Door. Communion was performed with water and scraps of stale bread.

In 1987, I was so stricken at not being allowed to send a Christmas message to my loved ones that I began madly pounding my head against the wall. With blood running down my forehead, I was pulled away by a guard, who chained me to a wall. In another moment of darkness, I prayed for hope. My guard brought me a newspaper. It carried a photo of some schoolchildren presenting my sister, Peggy, a birthday card they had made for me. The glimpse of those children was a great comfort.

To help preserve my sanity I saved matchsticks and wire to make a crucifix. When guards tossed me a set of Muslim prayer beads, I rethreaded them into a rosary.

Some of my captors were noncommittal, others cruel. But there was one sadistic man I shall never forget: Ali. The pain he inflicted was mental. One night he announced, "You're all going home." In delirious excitement we began putting on the new clothes and shoes that were handed to us for "the bus waiting downstairs."

Nothing happened. Our captors took the clothes away, and we were left dumbfounded.

After almost seven years came my true day of release: December 4, 1991. Reporters asked if I could ever forgive my captors. I hesitated a moment. But then I remembered the Lord's Prayer: "Our Father . . . forgive us our debts, as we also have forgiven our debtors."

I answered, "Yes, as a Christian I am required to forgive, no matter how hard it may be."

I learned so much in those 2,455 days. For I believe pain can help us grow. Before my capture I was a brusque, arrogant, restless man. Now I like to think I have changed. I don't know what lies ahead; but whenever I need to know where my help will come from, I will recall an old church in an English town, and a worn red Bible. And I will remember what Joseph said in forgiving his brothers, who had sold him into captivity: "You meant evil against me; but God meant it for good" (Genesis 50:20, RSV).

LET SOMEONE ELSE BE THE JUDGE

JEAN STAPLETON

Jean Stapleton won three Emmy awards for her role as
Edith Bunker in the hit television series All in the Family.

hen I was growing up in New York City, there was one thing that I disliked with a passion and that was calf's liver. My father, an outdoor advertising salesman, loved calf's liver, and so my mother saw to it that it often appeared on our dinner table. I would rather go hungry—and often did—than eat it.

The interesting thing is, I never even tasted calf's liver until I was an adult. I simply disliked the looks of it and knew, beyond all argument, that I would despise it. Today I adore calf's liver.

It wouldn't surprise me at all if Archie Bunker hated calf's liver. If you know Archie from *All in the Family*, the television comedy series in which I played his dingbat wife, Edith, then you know what I mean. Archie's a bigot, a super bigot, and we got most of our laughs from his outrageous points of view, his rantings against other races and almost anything new or strange to him. If it's true that the bravest man who ever lived was the first fellow to eat an oyster, you have some idea of where Archie would rate for courage—and how he'd camouflage his fear with a loud tirade.

By being extreme, and therefore ridiculous and funny to us, Archie has made millions of people aware of the absurdity of prejudice. I have confessed to my own absurd dealings with liver because it points up something that I was aware of long before Archie came along: Prejudice is an assortment of deceptively small personal judgments—deceptive because of their great cost in our daily lives.

No one will ever know, for example, how many families have been racked by stubborn arguments over long hair. Is prejudice involved? Partly, I think, for at its root, prejudice is a matter of judging—of prejudging really. We have preconceived opinions that long hair means something about a boy (and therefore about ourselves, since he is our offspring) that may or may not be true.

For myself, I have seen how my own niggling, personal prejudgments often have robbed me of pleasure and peace of mind. There have been times when I have tried to cure these prejudices, and I recall one time in particular when a conscious effort at healing resulted in a crucial breakthrough in my acting career. It happened a long time ago, in the late 1940s, after a good many bleak years trying to crack Broadway. Those had been years of constant work, of having a job as a secretary in the shipping department of a railroad company by day; typing manuscripts late at night in exchange for drama lessons; begging time off for summer stock; making precious little progress.

Then one day the chance came to read for one of the Equity Library Theatre productions—shows that our actors' union put on to give us a chance to work and to be seen. The play was *The Corn Is Green*, and there were two roles in it I felt confident I could handle. One of them was so minuscule; however, that though I knew it meant a job, there was some doubt as to whether it would be a good showcase. Naturally the tiny part was the one I was offered.

I thought about it awhile. "I'll do it," I said finally, irritated that they hadn't given me the larger part.

Ten days before the opening, the actress rehearsing Mrs. Watty fell on some ice and broke her leg. I assumed that I would inherit her role and I wasn't surprised when Ted Post, the director, came to talk to me. He asked me if I would fill in until he could get somebody else.

"*Somebody else!* But what about me?" I protested. "I can play her."

"No," he said, "you're too young."

I couldn't believe him. He just was not being fair. He had it in for me.

I got angry. I got so mad that I couldn't even sit at the same dinner table with my parents that evening. I had to get up and go to my room and try to collect myself. I had to do something about this injustice or I would burst.

In those days—as well as today—I had my own way of finding help when needed. I took out my Bible. After all, I had been going to Sunday school classes in our church since the age of two. I also took out my concordance, that remarkable compilation of all the key words in the Bible and where they appear. I flipped through the pages of the concordance to the "J's," mumbling theatrically all the while, "Justice is what I need, justice. . . ." But before I could find "justice" my eyes fell on "judge."

"For the Lord is our *j.* Isaiah 33:22."

I picked up the Bible and sped to Isaiah. I had explored Scripture in this fashion many times before, sometimes losing myself for hours in random adventure. Now, chapter 33 . . . there it was. "For the Lord is our judge, the Lord is our lawgiver, the Lord is our king; he will save us" (KJV).

What was this I was asking about justice? Had I jumped to some emotional conclusion about Ted? Should I pray about this and try leaving justice to the Lord?

I prayed; I relinquished the matter to the Highest Power. My anger disappeared. I was back in the dining room for dessert.

The next day at rehearsal I was no longer driven by an ambition to play Mrs.

Watty. I read the part as well as I could and enjoyed doing it, and when Ted found somebody he thought was the right age, I retired with genuine grace.

But that wasn't the end of the story. Three nights later, the producer called me at home and said that the new Mrs. Watty hadn't worked out. If Ted should ask me, would I be willing to take over? Very quietly I told her I'd be delighted, and the next day Ted said, "You're too young for it, Jean, but the part's yours."

It's still not the end of the story. Just as all show business sagas ought to unfold, an important agent saw me at the opening. She wasn't fooled by my makeup. She saw me as a young woman, just right, she decided, for the role of the niece in a touring company of *Harvey*. Out of that came my first good job in the theater; I was on my way.

Today, when I get emotional about something I think somebody has done to me, I try to think back to that experience before I start hurling a few hasty, bigoted thunderbolts. I recall that I never succeeded in changing the director's opinion of me; nor did I change my own opinion. I had simply left the judging to the Lawgiver, and he decided for both of us.

A friend once sent me a sermon entitled, "God and Archie Bunker," written by the pastor of the Brentwood Presbyterian Church here in California. In that sermon, Dr. Spencer Marsh Jr., who enjoys Archie, nonetheless noted his self-centeredness, his cliché-ridden bravado, his imprisonment inside his own narrow opinions. He quoted some dialogue from the show, from the night Archie was talking to "our" son-in-law saying, "I've been making my way in the world for a long time, sonny boy, and one thing I know—a man better watch out for number one. It's the survival of the fittest."

Doctor Marsh said that Archie is out of position, that Archie is a mixed-up person "because the number one slot, which he claims, is reserved for God." He sees

Archie as the elder brother in Christ's prodigal son parable, the one who stands outside the house grumbling about his rights while the welcome-home party is going on inside. The walls that separate him from the party are self-imposed, self-righteous, judgmental ones.

That's one reason I worry about prejudice. It could keep me from the party. It could keep me from enjoying the company of other people and what they have to offer, just as surely as it almost kept me from the simple pleasure of calf's liver or, more important, the big break of my career.

And poor Archie, like a lot of us, never listens, never learns. He'll never know that by blindly pushing away the oyster, he might be missing its pearl.

THE ROCK OF MY LIFE

LIONEL HAMPTON

Jazz great Lionel Hampton played with Louis Armstrong and
Benny Goodman before forming the Lionel Hampton Orchestra in 1940.

When my wife Gladys died in 1971 I said to myself, "Hamp, you got to call it quits too." Gladys was such a big part of me that when she was gone, I swore I'd never play another note. For the thirty-five years of our marriage she was my business manager, my accountant; she arranged my bookings, my recording dates and gave me every kind of guidance I needed. Then, suddenly, she was gone.

For a while I didn't care much about anything at all. I'd just stare at her photograph all day while my vibes collected dust. I felt totally helpless without her. I didn't want to do anything and even felt like chucking away the biggest dream of my life—a housing project and music school I wanted so much to build in New York City.

This dream had really begun back in the 1940s. I had left Benny Goodman's band and had a group of my own. We would be playing a lot of one-nighters on the road and when we'd go into a southern town, I made a point of going to the presidents of the black colleges and asking why they had no courses in black music and its place in American history.

"That's all behind us," was the usual answer I got.

Well, to me it may have been behind us, but I knew the importance black songs had to this country; and I wanted people to understand how the gospels and blues rose up out of the cotton fields and plantations. I wanted to tell how blacks, through their music, had created an identity for themselves.

While the college presidents weren't interested, my idea stayed with me for the next twenty years. In the 1960s, I managed to get together some pretty important cats to rap seriously about my dream. They included the presidents of several colleges and the head of the New England Conservatory of Music. I told them I wanted to teach not only the works of Bach and Mozart but also have students study great black musicians like Art Tatum, Fats Waller, Fletcher Henderson and, of course, Louis Armstrong. The school, we decided, would be built in New York's poverty-stricken Harlem section, an area that I had lived in for thirty years. I was also going to teach there and later we would expand into law and business programs.

When I first took our idea to the Harlem community leaders, their response was, "We need housing first, man. Get us this, and you'll get your school."

Spurred on, I immediately went to work. About $750,000 was raised from local sources. The governor offered his help and so did the federal housing authorities. However, much more money was needed, for the plan called for three apartment towers—over 355 apartments in all, plus a day-care center, a clinic and then my school. On paper it was something I could really dig, like something dropped from heaven.

I kept working on the plans and the money, right up until Gladys died. Then I shelved it. It didn't seem to hold me anymore—nothing did. All I could seem to do was think of her and how I missed her. I turned into one sour song.

Then, to add to my woes, the housing project began to run into trouble. Many of the Harlem residents were unhappy that whites were going to do much of the construction work, and that even some whites would be going to the school. The hatred started to rise and I didn't know how to deal with it. We needed the knowledge of the whites and we needed them at the school. Harlem, though, can be a bitter place—some residents were even threatening to tear my complex down if it were ever built.

One evening I sat at home, alone and discouraged. I wondered what Gladys would have advised. How I wished she were there to give me some answers! Then I thought about how close Gladys and I were, and how in our closeness we had shared many things—tastes in music, food, friends, shows. We would also share our worries. In fact, that evening I remembered what Gladys usually said when I had a problem.

"Dear," I could hear her say, "let's forget our troubles tonight and rub them out by reading the Psalms."

We often shared the reading of many of the Psalms. Gladys' favorite was Psalm 40, the second verse in particular, and there were several nights when she would read it to me and vice versa. There was such a great pleasure in that Psalm for me that I turned to it on a night when I thought I couldn't possibly go on. I took my Bible and went over and sat on the sofa that Gladys had recovered herself, and read the second verse. I read it over and over: "He brought me up also out of an horrible pit, out of the miry clay, and set my feet upon a rock, and established my goings" (KJV).

This seemed to be a turning point. Soon after that, I got what seemed like a new burst of energy. I was strong all of a sudden, like after a four-bar rest. I wrote letters to all sorts of people, pushed the architects, and gave talks on my dream. Soon, money began pouring in. We were nearing our goal.

One day I found myself up near the building site, talking with Harlemites about the racial trouble on the project. "Look," I told them, "it's just like in music—you got to have the white keys as well as the black ones to make harmony."

Somehow they bought this, and the hatred began to fade, maybe because, as one fellow said to me later, "It was your enthusiasm, Hamp, that hooked us." Black workers were now eagerly looking forward to getting some great on-the-job training there from whites.

Finally, on November 21, 1971, I knew I had, through God's help, pulled myself out of the horrible pit I had been stuck in.

On that day we held a ground-breaking ceremony in Harlem. I jammed for a big audience that morning and made some speeches and got a lot of tears in my eyes. It was all too good to be true. What made me proudest though, was telling everyone that when the buildings were completed there would be a motto nailed up out front. The motto, I said, was one that was very close to me now. It was that old second verse of Psalm 40: He "set my feet upon a rock, and established my goings."

AT THE FOOT OF THE CROSS

ERNEST BORGNINE

Ernest Borgnine's role in From Here to Eternity *propelled him into a career that has spanned more than fifty years and includes both film and television.*

Back in 1975 I was offered a part in the film *Jesus of Nazareth*, which through the years has been shown at Easter time on NBC television. Our cast, directed by the renowned Franco Zeffirelli, included Anne Bancroft as Mary Magdalene, and Olivia Hussey as Mary, mother of Jesus. I played the part of the centurion who was present at the crucifixion, the one whose servant had been healed by Jesus.

Much of the film was shot in Tunisia on the Mediterranean during January and February of 1976. A cold, damp wind continually knocked over floodlights and stung us with desert sand. I was uncomfortable in my thick leather uniform. My neck ached under a ponderous metal helmet, and I even began to pity those ancient Roman soldiers who were called centurions because they commanded one hundred men.

When it came time for my scene during the crucifixion, the weather was chill and gray. The camera was to be focused on me at the foot of the cross, and so it was not necessary for Robert Powell, the actor who portrayed Jesus, to be there. Instead, Zeffirelli put a chalk mark on a piece of scenery beside the cameraman. "I want you to look up at that mark," he told me, "as if you were looking at Jesus."

"Okay," I said, moving into position and looking up at the mark as instructed. "Ready?"

I hesitated. Somehow I wasn't ready. I was uneasy.

"Do you think it would be possible for somebody to read from the Bible the words Jesus said as He hung on the cross?" I asked.

I knew the words well from the days of my childhood in an Italian-American family in Connecticut, and I'd read them in preparation for the film. Even so, I wanted to hear them now.

"I will do it myself," Zeffirelli said. He found a Bible, opened it to the book of Luke and signaled for the camera to start rolling.

As Zeffirelli began reading Christ's words aloud from Luke 23, I stared up at that chalk mark, thinking what might have gone through the centurion's mind.

That poor Man up there, I thought. I met him when he healed my servant, who is like a son to me. Jesus says he is the Son of God, an unfortunate claim during these perilous times. But I know he is innocent of any crime.

"Father, forgive them; for they know not what they do." The voice was Zeffirelli's, but the words burned into me—the words of Jesus.

Forgive me, Father, for even being here, was the centurion's prayer that formed in my thoughts. I am so ashamed, so ashamed.

"Verily I say unto thee, Today shalt thou be with me in paradise," said Jesus to the thief hanging next to him.

If Jesus can forgive that criminal, then he will forgive me, I thought. I will lay down my sword and retire to my little farm outside of Rome.

Then it happened.

As I stared upward, instead of the chalk mark, I suddenly saw the face of Jesus Christ, lifelike and clear. It was not the features of Robert Powell I was used to seeing, but the most beautiful, gentle visage I have ever known. Pain-seared, sweat-stained, with blood flowing down from thorns pressed deep, his face was still filled with compassion. He looked down at me through tragic, sorrowful eyes with an expression of love beyond description.

Then his cry rose against the desert wind. Not the voice of Zeffirelli, reading from the Bible, but the voice of Jesus himself. "Father into thy hands I commend My spirit."

In awe I watched Jesus' head slump to one side. I knew he was dead. A terrible grief welled within me, and completely oblivious to the camera, I started sobbing uncontrollably.

"Cut!" yelled Zeffirelli. Olivia Hussey and Anne Bancroft were crying too. I wiped my eyes and looked up again to where I had seen Jesus—he was gone.

Whether I saw a vision of Jesus that windswept day or whether it was only something in my mind, I do not know. It doesn't matter. For I do know that it was a profound spiritual experience and that I have not been quite the same person since. I believe that I take my faith more seriously. I like to think that I'm more forgiving than I used to be. As that centurion learned two thousand years ago, I have found that you simply cannot come close to Jesus without being changed.

WHAT'S THE WORST YOU CAN IMAGINE?

MARY ELLEN CLARK

Two-time Olympic medalist Mary Ellen Clark is the oldest
women's diving medalist in the history of the Olympics.

iving is my passion, my life. I've been doing it since I was a kid, starting out with somersaults on the trampoline in our backyard in Newton Square, Pennsylvania, and quickly graduating to the springboard of our neighborhood pool. My dad, who worked for IBM, had been a diver at the University of Pennsylvania. I attended Penn State, where I became a platform diver. A ten-meter platform is as high as a three-story building. You hit the water like a bullet. My first time on the platform it took me a half hour standing at the edge before I got up the nerve to dive. I've never looked back. The exhilaration of arcing out into thin air, turning a three-and-a-half somersault, then slicing into the water is nearly indescribable to anyone who hasn't done it.

If you asked a scriptwriter to concoct the worst condition that could afflict a competitive diver, a really imaginative scenarist might come up with vertigo. Of the three divers I've heard of who have battled vertigo, none was able to continue diving. In 1995, with the Atlanta Olympic Games fast approaching, I was diagnosed as vertiginous, and I was scared.

It had first happened in 1988 at the Southern Cross meet in Australia. During one of my preliminary dives, I knifed into the water only to find myself disoriented. I had hit fine, my classic rip entry; it had been a good dive. But while thrashing around in the green murk, I wasn't able to determine which way was up. I wear contacts, so I have to keep my eyes closed underwater. I swam, not knowing which direction I was going. Finally I broke the surface, gasping. When I hoisted myself out of the pool, everything was spinning like a carousel. What was happening to me?

Contrary to popular impression, vertigo is not necessarily caused by fear of heights. Dizziness and loss of balance are the symptoms, and there can be many causes and triggers. But vertigo is the last thing you want to suffer while standing on the high-dive platform. I struggled with it on and off for five months, not even knowing what was wrong or what the name for my problem was, before it mysteriously cleared up. I said a prayer of thanks and tried to forget about it. It returned in 1990, disappeared in a couple of days, and I thought I was through with it forever.

By then I had graduated from Penn State, earned a master's in physical education from Ohio State, and, with Dad's encouragement, moved to Florida to train with legendary diving coach Ron O'Brien. Coach O'Brien said I stood a chance of making the 1992 U.S. Olympic team that would compete in the Barcelona summer games. It would be a dream come true. "I know you can do the work," Coach O'Brien encouraged me.

Training was grueling. You can't dive off the platform every day. The impact of hitting the water at high velocity again and again takes its toll on the body. But all the training was worth it. When I was named to the U.S. Olympic Diving Team I called back to Newtown Square immediately: "I made it, Dad!"

Though I had good news that summer, Dad had some bad. He was scheduled for open heart surgery. My first impulse was to skip the Olympics so I could stay with him. Dad wouldn't hear of it. "After all, Mare," he reassured me, "isn't this what I got you started on? Remember?"

Through all my years of competition, one image I kept close was that of my dad bending me into the proper dive position on the springboard when I was little.

Now, hugging me good-bye before I left for Barcelona, my dad said, "I'll be watching you on TV, Mare." Dad, who had taken all seven of us children to church every Sunday, kept a strong faith that would sustain him through whatever lay ahead. On the plane I prayed and received the strong impression he would be all right.

Soon I was faced with another dilemma: the opening ceremonies were scheduled to take place between 8:00 P.M. and 1:00 A.M. the night before my first event. I would get only a few hours sleep if I marched with the other U.S. Olympians. "We can always watch it on TV back at the Olympic village," Coach said.

I recalled my Dad's words: "I'll be watching you on TV." I had gotten word he had come through his surgery nicely and was recovering well. It would make him so proud to see me with the other Americans. So I marched, the only platform diver at the ceremonies. After the next day's competition I was in second place, a dark horse for a medal. The Russian and Chinese divers had been heavily favored. At twenty-nine, I had been written off by most people as too old to win.

"Maybe you should march before all your events," Coach joked.

But my next-to-last dive was a disaster and plunged me into fifth place. I had one final shot at a medal. As I stood on the platform ready to take my last dive, I paused a bit longer than usual to savor the moment.

A gentle Mediterranean breeze ruffled the air. The crowd was silent. I patted myself dry with a chamois as the announcement came over the loudspeaker. "Mary Ellen Clark of the United States, doing a backward one-and-a-half somersault with two-and-a-half twists."

I tossed the chamois away. It wrapped itself nicely around the railing of a lower board. Good shot, I thought. I stepped up to the edge of the platform and turned my back to the water. With a quick prayer and an incredible sense of lightness I was airborne, arcing out over the pool, twisting and tumbling, the Barcelona skyline flashing by. A micro-instant later I ripped into the water. I knew I had nailed the dive. When I shot back to the surface Coach O'Brien was yelling, "Bronze, Mary Ellen, bronze!"

As I stood on the awards platform to accept my medal, I knew Dad was watching. This is for you, Dad, I thought. What an incredible feeling!

In 1995, I was training again with Coach O'Brien for the '96 Summer Olympic Games in Atlanta. January 18 was just another practice day at Fort Lauderdale's International Swimming Hall of Fame. I had kept up a full schedule of competitions since I won the bronze in Barcelona, and I was in the best shape of my life. I took a quick springing step off the one-meter board and did a simple practice dive. As soon as I hit the water I knew something was wrong.

This time I consulted a slew of specialists. An EKG ruled out an organic brain disorder. One doctor thought it was an inner ear problem. Another suspected a virus. One thing was agreed on: I had vertigo, and it would be madness to continue diving. I had to withdraw from the Pan-American Games that winter.

I was confused and distraught. Would I ever dive again? For a while I slept with a cervical collar, sitting up in a chair. I tried acupuncture. I saw a nutritionist. I tried Eastern remedies like ginkgo biloba, rhubarb, cinnamon twigs, oyster shell, and ginseng, not to mention any number of Western pharmaceutical drugs. Still, I got horribly dizzy. Sometimes it even happened when I stood up too fast. Then *Sports Illustrated* magazine reported that "the best female diver in the country cannot dive because she is dizzy."

One night I found myself wailing out my problems on the phone to Steve DuVall, a friend whose spiritual strength I greatly admire. Finally Steve cut me off. "Mary Ellen," he said, "what is the worst possible scenario you can imagine?"

"That I'll never dive again."

"Can you accept that?" he asked.

I hung up without arriving at a definite answer. As I leaned back in my chair I thought of the Apostle Paul's words: "I have learned the secret of being content in any and every situation, whether well fed or hungry, whether living in plenty or in want. I can do everything through him who gives me strength" (Philippians 4:12-13, NIV).

The question was, could I *not* do something through him who gives me strength? Could I not dive again and find contentment? And at that moment I realized my father and mother had given me something more important than diving— they had given me faith. It was a part of me that went all the way back to when I was a little girl and was taught trust in God is the most important thing of all. Isn't that what faith is? Trusting in God? As much as I loved my sport, I knew I could go on without it as long as I had my faith, as long as I trusted and persevered. The rest was up to God.

Eventually I found relief from vertigo with the Upledger Institute's Craniosacral Therapy. In a strange way, I think vertigo has made me a better diver, a calmer and more focused athlete. It's given me a greater appreciation for the blessings I've had in my sport, and helped me see that life is more than competition and medals. Diving is still my passion, but it is tempered. Each time I leap off that thirty-three-foot platform I am reminded what trust and faith really mean.

AUTHOR INDEX

Title Index